ECHO'S FUGUE

21st CENTURY ESSAYS
David Lazar and Patrick Madden, Series Editors

ECHO'S FUGUE

Desirae Matherly

MAD CREEK BOOKS, AN IMPRINT OF
THE OHIO STATE UNIVERSITY PRESS
COLUMBUS

Library of Congress Cataloging-in-Publication Data

Cover design by Angela Moody
Text design by Juliet Williams
Type set in Adobe Garamond Pro

vox tantum atque ossa supersunt:
vox manet, ossa ferunt lapidis traxisse figuram.
inde latet silvis nulloque in monte videtur,
omnibus auditur: sonus est, qui vivit in illa.
—Ovid, *Metamorphoses,* Book III: l. 398–401

Only her voice and her bones remain: then, only
voice; for they say that her bones were turned to
stone. She hides in woods and is seen no more
upon the mountain-sides; but all may hear her,
for voice, and voice alone, still lives in her.
—Frank Justus Miller, translation (1916)

CONTENTS

ACKNOWLEDGMENTS

Many people made this work possible, through their guidance or support. Literary magazines and journals where the following essays appeared cultivated hope for an ambitious project: *Hotel Amerika,* "Fragments toward an Index of Birds"; *The Cossack Review,* "Mimesis"; and *ninthletter.com,* "Solo." My thanks to Tusculum, the school that puts food on my table, helps me attend conferences, fills my days with colleagues and students I admire and enjoy working with. I'm indebted to the humanities, for making life meaningful and also beautiful.

The mentoring and friendship of David Lazar has been a constant in my life for over two decades. His humor, style, and brilliance are unmatched, and if not for him I might never have met Montaigne. Patrick Madden continues to inspire me through his kindness and generous spirit. Both Pat and David have helped me stay focused and have taught me so much about the essay these many years. Writer friends kept me going through this long project, at points when I was ready to give up: Julija Šukys, Heather Elouej, Kelsey Trom, Wayne Thomas, Shannon Lakanen, John Yu Branscum. I'm grateful for editors, especially Kristen Elias Rowley, who has been a kind and stable presence from the beginning. My intern, Taylor Rose, and my ninth grade English teacher, Lesley Allen, for help with the sentence diagrams. Joshua Reimundo Gonzalez and Jamie Matherly, for catching my unwilling shadow. Deep gratitude for my family, but most of all, Sullivan Martin: chief encourager, rice maker, tea master, super kid, and sometimes editor. You are my heart.

naturally coalesced into something reasonably whole and unified. In the case of these essays, the structure preceded the first essay, and when barely begun I was working to harmonize two parts of my life that had always been present—music and love: two unimaginably broad themes that I felt could be endlessly generative in my desire to recreate J. S. Bach's *Art of Fugue* in prose form.

Writer-friends knew I was working with fugues and sent links to resources. Most notably, my brother in the essay, Patrick Madden, sent me a quotation of Théophile Gautier's, sometime in 2013:

> The arithmetic is in existence: we have not to invent it; we have only to learn it. One must learn to be at home in fugue and counterpoint, and to render one's talent supple and limber by the gymnastics of words.

The second sentence immediately became an imperative to think about the connections between musical composition and the composition of prose. A couple of years later, I stumbled upon the same quotation in his alchemical collection of essays, *Sublime Physick*. In the essay "Independent Redundancy" Madden explores "a term [he] invented to describe the phenomenon of two or more individuals coming up with the same idea without any cross-pollination or shared influence."[1] The essay explores many significant instances in music where this has happened, but also finds the larger truth of art and life: the endless recycling of human material into something both old and new, both original and bearing a resemblance.

I'd like to stay with the ideas that Madden raises in this particular essay, because I thought about some parts of it in a similar but still very different way for the four years I studied fugue. Madden—whom I know more easily as Pat—worked on "Independent Redundancy" seven years, and I know the pain of working on an essay for what feels an interminable time. I have one nearly that long in gestation that I cannot ever bring myself to finish because of the darkness of the theme. But Pat's essay, in his lighthearted, characteristically familiar, and quotidian way, considers every aspect of originality, including synesthesia, which is the best sort of associative alchemy there is. He writes:

And if those combinations arrive across merged senses? If Schubert heard E minor and saw "a maiden robed in white with a rose-red bow on her chest," if Beethoven struck D major and visualized shocks of brazen orange, if Kandinsky unfurled a ribbon of blue across his canvas and saw the infinite, then shouldn't I at least try?

I love this question because he asks it of himself, and in doing the particular of it, asks the question for all of us. Don't we all experience a degree of synesthesia, as artists of one medium or another? Don't we all take inspiration from each other, and from every form of expression? In a fantastically rich quotation that Pat records of Kandinsky's, wherein he compares color to the keyboard and claims "the soul is a piano with many strings," I'm delighted by the ways my friend reminds me that this is just one among near infinite ways we absorb and refashion our aesthetic environment. But back to finding Théophile Gautier in this expansive essay—I see Pat has captured what I'd been exploring through fugue:

> I have learned that no matter the seeming preplottedness of my nonfictional subject matter, I must write in thrall to the rhythms and sounds inherent in the linguistic medium I employ to re-create experience. In other words, I care less about telling a story the way it happened and more about making a kind of music from story.

I like this idea very much, though I want to add that coincidence works into this matrix for me, and there has never been a time when I didn't find signs all around me of what I need (encouragement, resources, guidance) precisely at the intersection of my awareness.

One example: At the Association of Writers & Writing Programs Conference in 2013, while walking from the Green Line to the Hynes Convention Center, I passed a building with the word "FUGUE" spray-painted above it. I took a picture, then less than an hour later (Friday, 9 a.m.) enjoyed a panel wherein Paul Lisicky spoke about fugue.[2] I experienced that shiver of familiarity whenever one writer realizes a shared thematic connection, perhaps not unlike what a Lover might experience when encountering someone who has shared a Beloved, but at a different time. This is perhaps extreme to say, but sometimes I think I finish essays just because I want others to know I've been working on them. Hard to admit, I also sometimes read the work of others half out of concern that we have inadvertently created that same "independent redundancy" that Patrick Madden explores. And to me, the redundancies more often have the feel of a coincidence, a literal co-incidence, but are probably the product of overidentification with particular qualities in one's environment. Like being at the intersection in a large city and seeing the one word that has become an obsession, noticing only later the captured clock in the foreground.

: :

Even as I began to plumb the idea of an essay for every fugue in Bach's masterpiece, I recognized that exploration of form was vitally important to this project. As Bach himself aimed at using a single music theme, or subject, to illustrate the potentialities of fugue structure, I hoped to do the same through prose. Although at first fugue seemed just a single, unifying passion, I cannot pretend that attempting this mimicry wasn't hubris, especially now, as I work to finalize the last essay that I know will ultimately fail to be comprehensive and will not finish or be resolved. Given that Bach's final piece in *The Art of Fugue* was likewise unfinished, I feel that this inclination toward all that is late and anticlimactic is requisite of any attempt to cover his great work, but beyond that aesthetic matter, I'm humbled by the recurrent epiphany that no monumental undertaking can ever be as comprehensive or as thorough as one would wish, nor can it adequately pay homage to all of the sources that went into its creation. I recall Pat's essay again: "All that we can hope for as essayists, it seems to me, is to have learned something of rhythm and pace and sentence carpentry from our predecessors, while gently leaving their particular styles behind, as a teenager tiptoes away from the college of her parents."[3]

Reader, I can ploy the trope of Montaignean preface as far as your patience will permit. I can plead that you not waste your time on something so frivolous, that you go outside and take in some of the blue sky that may or may not be the ceiling of your day. As I get older, I feel that I am less a reader than I am a thinker, and would rather be, truth be told, backpacking across the prehistoric spine of a mountain most days than indoors typing in front of a screen. But nevertheless, here we are, it is the end of a long year and this moment will fold into the next, and then the one after that, until everything is new again and I'm finally done with work that took six cycles to tend.

Bach was a lover of puzzles and games, and while learning about his composition process I found myself equally engaged by the opportunities to *play*, to make what I worked on more indicative of exercise than of flawless execution. What little we actually know about the man, Johann Sebastian Bach, is made up for by the enormity of his work that was really only appreciated long after his death. He seems to have been a hard worker; a lover of coffee, tobacco, and beer; and perhaps an amorous husband considering he fathered twenty kids. Only half of his children lived into adulthood, typical of his time. He knew something about loss. When I admit to having conversed with an imaginary Bach on New Year's Day 2012, I only mean that I had the peculiar sense that he was with me that morning, and I had great fun imagining his frequent visitations after that, as ludicrous as they might seem in hindsight. I decided that Bach's dexterous hands probably made him one hell of a gamer, and I imagined coming home after having been at work all day to a nacho chip-eating, 18th century North German engaged in marathon sessions on the Xbox. I also saw him wagging his finger at me whenever I shirked my writing duties. By the time I wrote our dialogue together, it occurred to me that a guru is no less real for lacking corporeality. I heard him, I saw him, and in whatever way we were linked, I could not deny that my only reason for mimicry was to honor him, and to learn what I could about composition, form, and his Magnum Opus, given that it is different for every individual who encounters it.

Stravinsky was a late-comer to my project. I felt that I had much more of Stravinsky's personality available to me, and so my imagination sought other ways to bring him into my world, to learn from him. I take greater liberties with Stravinsky's imagined persona than I do with Bach's, but this emerges as much from what his dissonant music invokes in my thinking as it does from his personal life, made intriguing by difficulty, patronage, and infidelity. As a writer, how faithful am I required to be to him, when reconstructing and editing his words or personality? In a popular film a great actor performs a famous character posthumously, through the miracle of digital innovation. Advertisers use computer generated avatars to sell us our idealized desires. Anyone who writes historical fiction resurrects or creates someone who existed beside those who do not. A song's covers become more famous and enduring than the initial recording. A machine composes new music in the style of the dead composer.[4] In retrospect, whatever life is breathed into Stravinsky's words so many years after their delivery are meant to extend his influence, given that the original context for them has evolved. To find a new context for everything, to make it new even if it no longer is—this seems a noble undertaking for any artist. I hope that any use of his work will encourage recognition of the ways one area of art influences another.

The timing of Stravinsky's entrance into the essays is also especially relevant, considering that I was questioning the sustainability of serial monoamory, and uncovering a possible narcissist (or becoming one), while dabbling in reading about game theory. Stravinsky and Bach seem to be polar opposites, both in terms of their music and their personal lives. In game theory, the "Bach or Stravinsky?" paradigm is alternate nomenclature for the game strategy known as "Battle of the Sexes." The clickpoint of the correspondence was too delicious to pass up as a culminating question, given that I was finding the end of my belief in romantic love. The "Battle of the Sexes" for me becomes the competition between two expressions of human sexuality: the monoamorous (monogamous) and the polyamorous. I cannot pretend to have been successful in this last matter, especially given that my understanding of game theory is limited. But I do ask the question that seems appropriate to this late age of posteverything, with all of time and the humanities undergoing revelatory and apocalyptic fits: what is my ethical obligation to love others, when I cannot count on anything (or anyone) to stay the same for long?

.

BLUEPRINT

I. Exposition

When Bessie Smith sings "'Tain't Nobody's Bizness If I Do" in a 1923 recording, I belt out the lyrics along with her, right up until the lines "I'd rather that my man would hit me / Than to just rise up and quit me." When she confesses, "I swear I won't call no copper / If I'm beat up / By my papa," I pause. Having lived in an unhappy marriage once, I told no one the fear I felt then.

I saw a lamp poised over my face, felt his hand around my throat, but it was years before I called the police, came to know how humiliating it was to explain my busted kitchen door, and endured the stigma of police cars in my driveway at 6 a.m. on an Easter morning. Though I was never "beat up," I sympathize with Bessie Smith's insistence that none of it is anyone's business and that she could manage just fine.

Blues songs, however much they may circle and repeat, still manage to convey in few words a suffering much greater than the sum of their lyrics. Though most blues songs seem rooted in suffering that we associate with heartbreak, loss, or abuse, many varieties of blues interpretations surpass pain, and ultimately praise the depth of the human soul. At least I think this, when I'm trying to explain why the blues are important to me, a child of working-class Appalachia, a white woman and single mother with an advanced degree. What do I know of the blues, and of Black lives and voices in a time not my own? Nothing I can pretend to.

I am no scholar of music, nor do I play any instrument well. In fact, I hesitate to call myself any kind of scholar at all though I am a professor at a small liberal arts university. All I know is my own human experience with music, and how it sometimes sealed me apart from the world, and how it also pulled me out of pain so deep I might have killed myself. All kinds of music. When I was a preteen, it was classical music that gave me an anchor. In the '90s, grunge was able to articulate my freshly adult angst. I've been through many gauntlets of sound since then, and now, the unlimited options overwhelm me. I shiver with the echoes of all the songs I've loved. The songs I've made love to. The songs I've nursed a broken heart with. The songs that helped me fall in love with other people who could not love me back.

I have spent a long time alone. Of the past twenty-four years, I've spent ten of those years in some state of heartbreak. I've tried the usual solutions: alcohol, religion, running, yoga, online dating. All I can say is that I am no closer to figuring out why I must want to be alone. Why else would anyone commit to the self-sabotage, the repetitive error of unrequited or halfway love if there were not the illusion that one could escape it? Maybe that's why I love the blues. There is the semitone of happiness and of despair. Nothing is too delightful unless it also bears the possibility of loss.

: :

Listening to music, like writing, is a way to relieve anxiety. In my own case—as someone who cannot play but studied music theory and tried piano, violin, guitar—the pseudo-accidental death of my father when I was five years old set into motion a whole range of anxieties that I've perennially worked out in essays. Initially I wrote out of irrational guilt, of the sort a child fashions after a divorce followed close by the death of the parent least understood, the least known. "Daddy" became the man I refer to in the deep past tense as my "father." I guess it was the loss of that ease by which I related to men through this one man in particular. It seems for all of my life I've been looking for the complexity and the intensity of a single relation that could surpass the genetic hold of my parentage. To be both longing for and embattled with half of my composition is the only thing worse than loss. Funny how often I've confused the two, desire and surrender.

I've always tended to fall in love with the wrong people. When I say "fall in love," I mean quickly—severely—desperately. I know it's a hard loving because my grandmother once said to me, "Baby, you love too hard." She was right, and she knew what loving too hard meant, since she loved my grandfather that way for thirty-seven years. She never remarried after her divorce, and never wanted to date. I tried that for a while myself, but four years after my worst heartbreak as an adult, I was willing to try it all again. Except that time, I wanted to believe I wasn't repeating myself. I look back now and see how naïve I was, how perfectly complicit I was with the pain that I was entering into. I had no idea how it would carry me from not one, but into three relationships that gradually wore me down. Here I am—six years after that first moment—admitting the error, the extraordinary and beautiful error of falling in love again. I can't help it. Here I go repeating myself, an echo in a chamber of hearts, my own heart, beating against the sides again, asking to be let in or out, I'm not sure. Either way, like a miser, I care what it costs.

Repeating myself feels like mistaken originality. Tending to never repeat words in a document, I search for cycles and correct them during second or third read-throughs. Recently, I used a form of the word "consider" twice in the final paragraph of a letter. No other word seemed to work, and I deliberated over synonyms until I chose the lesser evil. *Repetitive,* I scrawl over specific words or entire sentences in student papers. *Kill the rhyme,* I tell another, when a word in a sentence repeats the sound signature of a previous sentence. More and more I become the maternal English professor with silvering hair and dowdy skirts. I look at myself naked in the mirror and see a woman failing to pretend. It isn't that my breasts aren't heavy or that my waist isn't smaller than my hips. I still have what some man might believe he wants in his mind or in his bed. It's just that I ask too much of Narcissus, who seems to become every man that I love. I want his attention but all I can say is what he has already said to himself. I speak, and it's just an echo of his desire, not mine. Why am I still standing alone in front of this mirror?

: :

My obsession for variance and progression apply to my musical tastes as well as my tastes for everything else. I might complain that I'm alone, but my real problem is that I'm unlikely to be satisfied by the same thing every day. I get bored easily. I tire of a man who wants me to praise him continuously. Soon, I begin to notice the oil in his hair, or the hole in his shirt, his soft—or conversely—bony frame. I have flaws of my own, but I begin to realize how unlikely it is that I could ever adore any one person endlessly, especially when I'm not altogether certain I'm the first on his mind either. My mind wanders, and I begin to move, to look around. What is it I want? Passion? Affection? Security? Or someone perennially new?

I am likewise intolerant of music that doesn't move me, either through lyrics, rhythm, melodic changes, or chord progressions. Songs that serve as exceptions are experiments in counterpoint, as in Johann Sebastian Bach's 1751 posthumous work, *The Art of Fugue,* whereby a single melody is rearranged fourteen different ways. On the surface—or to the disinterested ear—fugue may sound like repetition. Its etymology is curious, as "fugue" is derived from the Latin *fuga* from *fugere,* meaning "to flee" and *fugare,* "to chase." Psychology uses "fugue state" to describe temporary amnesia, and despite this, I see fugue as the metaphor of my repetitious and unconscious errors, which are easily and too painfully remembered. "Fugue," like "cleave," is an auto-antonym, or a contranym; that is, a word that means its opposite. People also contain their own opposite forces within them—that is, the potential for internal consonance or dissonance—the counterpoint of existence. And yet—the fugue as form, much of classical music, much of what is referred to as "the blues"—sounds repetitive. I hope I don't sound like a cretin when I admit this.

It isn't that I don't know the appeal of repetition. Desperately, I try love again and again, hoping I know enough about myself to not repeat the error, perhaps of loving someone who does not, or cannot love me back. I try to be realistic, accept that everyone encounters the same kinds of self-judgments: of not feeling attractive enough, of not feeling deserving of love. Among my worries early into my adult life was that musicians would always attract me, and that relationships with them were impossible. They were too easily moved, too fluid, too permissive emotionally. But that wasn't it. I tried loving scholars, soldiers, and martial artists. They each whistled some tune or another and I answered back with an echo, an endless ear of a canyon or mountain face. Perhaps I just wanted the sex. Maybe it was enough to feel desirable for a while. But something in me resists the permanence of a long-term relationship and I've tried blaming its absence on everyone else for most of my life.

My first love was a jazz drummer, and whenever I hear Wilco's refrain in "Heavy Metal Drummer" (2002), I'm reminded of a culminating moment in a friend's college dorm room, when I finally realized what kind of friendship we had and acknowledged that high school was over. All analysis aside, I spent an embarrassing evening alone one night with a bottle of wine, leaving a message (or two? three?) on his answering machine. (Echo calling.) Years after that, in our small town, a mutual friend ran into him. She said that he remorsefully muttered, "Desi must hate me." I didn't then, and I don't now, though I regret having believed in him at the expense of myself. As Wilco sings, "I miss the innocence I've known," I realize I don't know how many drunken nights I've suffered through since then. Surely we stop counting at such-and-such age. Here I am many years later, almost thirty years later, not drinking or crying much, but certainly aware of the repetition of pain, its reverberations in my hollowed heart.

: :

Repetition is tolerable in other aspects of my life. I like villanelles, for instance. During a visit to the college where I teach, poet Allison Joseph characterized the villanelle as the perfect poetic form for writing out obsession. Generally, I tend toward obsession, to the point that I sometimes talk to myself. I repeat, in these private admonitions: *Let it go let it go let it go* or *I'm done I'm done I'm done* . . . It's admissible then, to mantra my way through a repetition that I hope will break some other, more serious repetitive force in my life, perhaps a habitual preoccupation or compulsion, like worrying needlessly, or pining over a love unreturned. Most of the time the two accompany one another; I obsess about whether I should be direct, I obsess about my past mistakes. My essays circle around and around one thing, one idea, one worry, (sometimes a passel of worries). At my best, I believe that most things progress spirally, wending through advancing, concentric whorls. But the direction sometimes changes, moving in retrograde motion. I go back before I go forward, and when I go back, I'm circling pain.

Sometimes I just like the familiarity of memory. I remember how it felt when he pushed me against the kitchen table, how right it felt when he lifted my skirt and pressed my face against the table top. Who cares how it ended months later? The moment was real. And then there was another man, the intensity of his gaze, the heaviness of his body, but much heavier, his misery. One after another they all added up to another reason for moving forward with my solitary life, even as I admit I haven't always wanted to. Will I ever feel happiness with someone again? And for once, will the feeling stay? Maybe it's obsessive to circle the past, but I think we all do it to some extent.

: :

The blues can be obsessive, repeating (repeating) a phrase over and over again; chord progressions of such monotony, that only by comparing variations do we hear differences. Artists whose lives are marked by loss and suffering may not necessarily address pain head on, but instead allude to it. In an abstraction, blues songs exist within their many variations as if they were parts of a larger fugue, the structure of subject, response, divertissement, coda. One song may be the original subject, each variation becoming the counter-subject, or response. From here, any later rendition that strays far from the original subject becomes much like an episode, or divertissement. I wager that the version we find most gratifying among all others generates a coda that only we can hear.

Big Maceo's "Worried Life Blues" (1941) insisting "But someday baby / I ain't going to worry my life anymore"; Muddy Waters's 1955 "Trouble No More": "But someday baby / You ain't gonna trouble poor me / anymore"; and Mississippi Fred McDowell's "Someday Baby" (1965) "You ain't gonna worry my life" are all versions of the same song, essentially. The "anymore" is impossible to discern in the first iteration of the repetitive line in McDowell's version, and yet it exists for anyone who knows the song well enough to hear it. Maybe an astute listener will discover what I didn't then—the original 1935 recording by Sleepy John Estes. What starts as a kind of country tune migrates to Chicago and reaches the Allman Brothers' live version on their 1972 album *Eat a Peach*. Who knows where this trouble ends? I listen to the song because I need to be reminded that whatever pain I feel now will not last forever. The desire slips away, like sound into the valleys, retreating away from its source, until it comes back in half-force, then in quarter-force, or some other ratio that echoes make. *Someday, Baby, I'm not going to fucking care. Someday, Baby, you're not going to even cross my mind.*

In early 2012 I (obsessively?) kept The Black Keys in heavy rotation. Their *Chulahoma* (2006) album covers several songs by master bluesman Junior Kimbrough. Comparing two recordings, such as "Have Mercy On Me" (Black Keys, 2006) and "Lord, Have Mercy On Me" (Kimbrough, 1994), shows that yes, they are the same song, but The Black Keys wait longer to introduce the vocals, while Kimbrough launches in shortly after half a minute. Kimbrough's version from *Sad Days, Lonely Nights* is almost ten minutes long, whereas The Black Keys take half that time to follow out the theme. Like sessions of lovemaking with two different partners, the songs differ in the ways each fulfills the desires of the listener. Through both, I want the moment to last as long as possible, even though I know they must each come to an end.

Junior Kimbrough's "Work Me Baby" (from *All Night Long*, 1992) is instrumentally sexier in the way it digs into my mind than The Black Keys's abbreviated "Work Me" (2006), though I confess a preference for the pulse of the bass and the percussion in the latter. The Black Keys's altered lyrics leave out Kimbrough's early lines, "If you love me / I will love you too" and the thrice repeated "We'll get together Baby / Make everything all right" (or "so good"). The Black Key's lyrics intensify the physical dimension of the song by altering the first iteration of "Till I want more" to "Baby work me / Till I won't look on." By imagining a man overwhelmed by "looking on," the subject of the song is established immediately, so that by the time we hear "Won't you do me / And Baby, I will do you too" we know in a direct way what the speaker desires, and "doing" does not suffer from any apparent imprecision. I'll admit preferring the loving relation over the physical, as if it could promise a longer term of pleasure and security. I should know by now this is impossible. I replay the song (replay . . . replay) just as I replay the scenes in my head of the last time I was loved. Which was better? Just different versions.

II. Divertissement

Over a decade ago, when I loved . . . I absorbed everything about him—the smell of his skin, the color of his eyes, the feel of his body, taut and muscled. Once: I swear that I nearly passed out, leaned backward and fell off the bed—or floated—it's a matter of perspective. He was delighted that I had felt so much, that I had temporarily lost control, that my eyes rolled back into my head in *le petit morte,* "the little death." He nervously laughed, then asked me if I was okay. I had experienced something like levitation, and found myself painlessly on the wooden floor several feet away. That kind of love is what I miss, what I seek, what I long to replicate. It is worth repeating, again and again, just to get it right. Cursed as we are with the souls of gods, our bodies live by finding these harmonies, and by overcoming the central dissonance of being human: of failing repetitively, and that pain coming back to bruise us in animal bliss.

: :

Even within the same musician's works, you'll find variations, as if each performance of a blues song surpasses all previous recordings or variations. When interpreted by The North Mississippi Allstars a song might be fast and upbeat. But in four different R. L. Burnside recordings of the same song, each extending from three to five minutes, all are much slower, and in many ways, more distinctive. "Po Black Maddie" (North Mississippi Allstars, 2000) and "Poor Black Mattie," (R. L. Burnside from *Acoustic Stories,* 1988) are clearly the same song; however, R. L. Burnside's is not as fast, and combines a breathy harmonica with the rhythmic strum. Of the two versions, I prefer his. With the blues, one song may come to surpass another in the way we expect the song to be sung, how we expect the guitar to be played, how it is paced, or how we feel when R. L. Burnside moans that he needs no fire because his woman is "cherry red." One man can carry different voices within his soul, which is how time inscribes the songs we sing. I'm forever finding and losing the belief that this can remain true, even after we've loved another, yet *another,* and lost.

: :

Circling pain seems to be in some way a definition of the blues. Every song in some way addresses loss, disillusionment, or desire. Though desire may not seem like a pain on first glimpse, anyone who has felt it sincerely down to the bone knows that it is. When you know you've been taken or deceived; when you've been cheated out of love or money; when no one will give you the chance you sorely need; when you desperately want to say something directly but it comes out in sly metaphor, you may be singing the blues. If you're planning on leaving your lover, if your lover has left you, or if someone else's lover has left someone else for you and you want to sing about it, you may be singing the blues. Regardless, in every case, you'll be repetitively strumming a progression of chords and echoing the call and response of old spirituals, asking anyone to hear you, to hear you, to hear you say where you're going, where you been, where you're leaving from, where you'll never go back to, and every variation on who, what, why, and how in these same configurations.

III. Development

My first serious boyfriend after my divorce played bass guitar, and in college had bandmates who eventually went on to play large venues. One day barely a month into our courtship, overcome by what was building between us, we pulled the car off alongside a hairpin turn on a mountain road and began to make out. When he whispered, *You're like music,* I wasn't thinking about words. Later I wondered: how? Because music is powerless against a hearer's evaluative interpretation? Or borrowing from Hamlet, was I an instrument on which he had learned the frets and stops?

When I would spend nights with him, he would hammer out bass lines that made me look on in loving admiration. But sometimes he'd catch a run of errors and self-punishing seconds would disrupt his playing. I watched him struggle to forgive himself for tiny mistakes, remembering my own resignation from violin in ninth grade, piano in high school, and guitar in college. For him to say I was "like music" was to say he'd always be too self-critical to compose our lives the way I wanted him to. Maybe I wasn't able to forgive my own neurotic errors either.

: :

When I was twenty-three, I married after a four-week-long courtship. Barely a week after marriage, I knew he was wrong for me. Six years later, I divorced without regret. When my boyfriend after my divorce said he was too busy to drive ten hours south to see me one summer, I ended a doomed long-distance engagement. In both cases, neither was the ideal, neither the one that could ever hurt me the same way my father had, by loving-then-leaving me. By this I judged my love: by the emptiness I felt in the long silences, deliciously free and undisciplined. What did I know?

After the death of a parent, when a child is too young to know about Oedipal complexes and how it is that people are born and die, it is sometimes easy to sustain the illusion that the deceased parent will return. I kept this illusion alive for at least a year if not more. But I think I also acquired a fixation on loving what is gone. Either this, or I decided to never love anyone who could go away from my life like that again. Or, I love in order to let go, again, once more, and yet again.

My father and my mother were passionate and jealous people, so it makes sense that I am the person that I am: divorced, often lonely, but protective of my solitary freedom. My mother says that no matter how much money they had, my father would buy a new album every week. She claims I was conceived during David Bowie's *The Rise and Fall of Ziggy Stardust* (1972) or Wings's *Band on the Run*

(1973). For a long time I believed my mother brought me into existence during David Bowie's "Soul Love" or better yet, "Five Years," since that's how long they lasted. It's impossible to know. David Bowie passes out of this world in the year I spend editing this essay. Whose birth or death is inscribed here? I watch the video for "Blackstar" and shiver when I recognize what appears to be choreography for Stravinsky's *Rite of Spring,* when the maidens circle the ritual virgin. It may be meaningless, unless I choose to see it as significant. I see all intersections of repetition as significant.

: :

My friendships were often built around music. My best friend was the one who introduced me to R.E.M., The B-52s, and The Beatles. It wasn't that I didn't hear enough of *The White Album* (1968) and *Abbey Road* (1969) growing up, but I'd never heard the earlier albums. I still remember a long school trip, when we were first becoming friends. She shared her earbuds with me on the bus, singing "In My Life" (1965) so perfectly, that I will forever hear her voice layering that track. Friendships that I have with other people almost always include music to some extent.

Some friendships exist only because of music, as if we can communicate intimately in that aspect only, as in the case of a former student I have exchanged albums with over the years. Music may be the only means of voicing the loss of something greater than what actually bonds us: the deaths of both our fathers. People withdraw into themselves, and into the inky cloud of music. Music speaks to us, as if only to us. And then, one day, I feel old. Cyclically, the music departs from my life, and there's no one I know who listens to the same music I do anymore. I'm alone, and what I play at home or in the car is meaningful only to me. Perhaps this is why I began attending music festivals in my late thirties: they provide a way of relating with strangers who will satisfy my need to never see them again, after having enjoyed something terrible, and beautiful, and real. How poignantly it mirrors the rest of my life.

: :

It was strangely satisfying to me, as a lonely child, to fantasize loving someone far away, maybe even long dead (Napoleon, Franz Liszt), and to have that love crushed beneath reality repeatedly. It's at least familiar, even if more than a little painful. I am drawn to men like my dead father: openly humorous, privately sad, stoic. I have reenacted the loss of my father many times, in different modes. Even if I am wrong, I cannot say that there is a lack of consistency with the manner in which my attainable loves have hurt me so badly I knew I must leave them first.

Though I have been repetitive in these romantic errors, there have been variations. I actually initiated the breakup with one serious long-distance boyfriend over the telephone, and a minute later began washing the dishes at my parents' house. A glass broke on my hand, so forcefully was I washing it, that I now carry a "C"-shaped scar (Cleveland? Chicago?) on my right thumb joint and had to have several stitches to pull my flesh together. After that night I was so doped up on painkillers that I didn't feel the first signs of a sorrow that would consume me for years afterward. When I say years, I mean at least five. During that time I gave up, because feeling nothing at all was preferable to the dangerous high of ecstasy and enjoyment, or the lows of trying to make him happy, as impossible as I know that desire to have been. Another feature of my short-lived loves—I'm attracted to unhappy men: those so abject they feel or pretend they can never be loved again. There's something delicious about the way they could reject me, even though I could be the last woman in the world to ever love them as they are, for who they are. It's confirmed then. I must be the abject one in each relationship. For by whom, and how . . . could I ever be loved?

IV. Coda

I sometimes crave the architecture of a family with a partner. I often desire the security that a happy marriage of equals can bring, and I long to forget disappointments. To say this means that I in part fear them, at least as much as I do any part of my past that composes me. I fear the possibility of blueprints, of plans drawn up by my psyche of structural failures and sabotages orchestrated by my own mind. I am afraid of myself, of my apparently cyclical passions, the lashings, the imprisonments, and the fallout of hasty decisions. I have caused my own unhappiness more often than I have been willing to admit.

I am more likely to repeat mantras, as a warning that all romantic love is a setup for despair. I trouble myself about the nature of love, I begin to gather old blues songs and listen, trying to find similarities, and then seek divergences. Though I was never so into the blues that I could listen to them for days on end, I am sometimes in that place where I would rather hear someone, perhaps Mississippi Fred McDowell, sing "Someday baby / You ain't gonna worry my mind," (1965) than think too much about where I'm always headed, through my own unconscious choosing.

I turn to The Rolling Stones, a band indebted to the American blues, and they remind me that wanting and needing are two different problems. Perhaps what we get is sometimes all that we deserve. In my fatalism, I recall needing the anchor that marriage brought, as well as the child who has sometimes been my only reason for the life I continue to live. Or, I recall with some gratefulness, the romance after my divorce that I so desperately enjoyed. Maybe I can't know what I need until it's gone, but I'm always trying to abandon that tired ideology. How to build from an old design? Here is the blueprint: it flutters, though there is no wind.

ECHO III

Whenever the goddess Juno went looking for her philandering husband, the nymph Echo would intentionally delay the goddess with mindless chatter. This is what Ovid tells us in his great work as a way of explaining the curse that led to her transformation. He tells us that she was once embodied before she wasted to only a voice. In his tale of Narcissus, Ovid relates the arrogance of the beautiful youth who attracted the attention of both sexes but spurned them equally. Narcissus was too full of himself, too in love with his own beauty, though we are not yet even to that part of the tale, and really, I simply want to talk about Echo. The poor wretch found Narcissus hunting in the forest and of course, fell in love. Cursed as she was, there was no way for her to make her advance toward him. Consider any number of women we might know who love men with whom they cannot or dare not assert themselves. Perhaps they revere their men too much, and themselves too little. Whatever afflicts these women is similar to what defined Echo. The grace of one who is too often alone, who walks softly on the earth lest she make a mark on it. She desired to be noticed, pursued, loved, but she withdrew into invisibility. Or worse, she loved unceasing despite abuse, never demanding nor expecting more. Thinking back, I wonder why Echo protected Jove. She did not seem to be among the nymphs he dallied with. Did she hope to win his attention by keeping watch? How then did Echo find herself a willing accomplice to adultery, with-

out promise of Jove's protection or mercy should Juno come calling? Perhaps she was always the voyeur, a silent spectator to the love
and desire of others. Men who wielded power in love that she could
never match. She could not have been other than what she was, before or after Juno's curse: a sad brittle flower on the fading wall.

ECHO II

Whenever   Juno went looking for her   husband,   Echo would intentionally delay the goddess with
      chatter. This is what Ovid tells us   as a
way of explaining the curse that led to   transformation.
      she was once embodied before she wasted to   a voice.
     of Narcissus, Ovid relates the arrogance of the
youth who attracted   both sexes but spurned them
     Narcissus was   too in love with his own
beauty, though we are not yet even to that   tale, and
I   want to talk about Echo. The   wretch found Narcissus
    in the forest and   fell in love. Cursed
there was no way   to make her advance   Consider
     women we   know who love men with whom
they   dare not assert themselves. Perhaps they revere their
men too much, and themselves too little. Whatever afflicts these
women is   what defined Echo   one
too often alone, who walks rarely on the earth lest she make a mark
    She desired to be   pursued, loved, but she withdrew
     Or worse, she loved   despite abuse, never
    expecting more.   I wonder why Echo
protected Jove. She did not seem to be among the nymphs he dallied with. Did she   win his attention by keeping watch? How
    did Echo find herself   accomplice to adultery, with-

out   Jove's protection   should Juno come calling? Perhaps she was   the voyeur, a   spectator to the
     desire of others. Men who wielded power   that she could
never match. She could not have been other than what she was,
          after Juno's curse: a sad brittle flower on the fading wall.

ECHO I

Whenever　　　　　　Juno went looking
　　　　　　Echo would　　　　　delay the goddess with
　　　chatter. This is　　　　　　　　　　　　a
way of explaining the curse that led to　　　transformation.
　　　she was once embodied before she wasted
　　　　　　　　　Ovid relates the arrogance of

　　　Narcissus　　　　　　　　　　　　in love with his own
beauty, though
I　　　want to talk about Echo. The　　　wretch found Narcissus
　　　in the forest and　　　　　fell in love. Cursed

　　　　　women　　　　　　　　　love men with whom
they　　　　dare not assert themselves. Perhaps they revere their
men too much, and themselves too little. Whatever afflicts these
women is　　　　　　what defined Echo
too often alone,　　　　　　　　　　lest she make a mark
　　　She desired to be　　　　　　loved,
　　　　　　　　　　　　　　despite abuse
　　　　　　　　　　　　　　　　Echo
protected Jove　　　　　　　among the nymphs he dallied with. Did she　　　win his attention by keeping watch?
　　　did Echo find herself　　　accomplice to adultery, with-

26

out   protection   should Juno come calling? Perhaps she was   the voyeur, a   spectator to the
     desire of   Men who wielded power   she could
never match. She could   have been other than what she was,
                    : a sad brittle flower   fading

ECHO

Whenever
        Echo would   delay   with
    chatter
        the curse   led to   transformation.
   she was once embodied before she wasted

           in love with
beauty
          Echo   found Narcissus
    in the forest and   fell in love. Cursed

      women   love

  too much
       what defined Echo
too often alone,
   She desired to be   loved

             Echo
        among the nymphs

   Echo   herself   accomplice to adultery, with-

out protection should Juno come calling she was the voyeur, a spectator to
desire who wielded power
She could have been other than
a sad flower fading

MIMESIS

1

Those who love unrequitedly know delusion: the mistaken belief, the myth that someone could provide the deserved love that one had always looked for and never found. At eighteen I began to slip from becoming the youthful optimist I'd never been. Always the bleak, painful failure to identify mutual love. I've dealt with delusion differently throughout my life. I was told about my father's death days after the funeral, because my mother was concerned that I would not be able to handle the reality. The result was something like a fugue state for me, and I still cannot remember that time after being told he'd "had an accident" in late July, until vacation in late August with my mother, uncle, and grandmother. Of flying to Denver through a turbulent storm, and travelling through Colorado, Wyoming, and the Dakotas in an RV: *Mountains, desert, plains.* At Fort Laramie's museum, my grandmother pulled me away from the bloodstained dress of a Sioux woman, the collar black-brown as if she'd been beheaded. I cried inconsolably, but then I was nearly six, preparing to enter first grade without a father. I must have remembered looking at his books about the American West, the sepia photos of American soldiers murdering whole family groups of indigenous men, women, children, and elders. I must have put it all together somehow: bloody death, decapitation, faces bludgeoned or blown open, living beauty deformed, lifeless, and lost. This was the moment my memory came back. I have since this time been afraid of forgetting, a fear that manifests itself through writing nonfiction, through essaying. I had forgotten the moments after I found out he was dead, of shouting something awful at my grandmother on the staircase, as if she had been to blame. I forgot where I went, or how I thought about what had happened. I began to forget his face. Maybe I *tried* to forget him. Maybe I forget him every day.

2

My divorce was in part brought about by my interest in another graduate student, ten years older than me and not particularly attractive, yet nonetheless charismatic. He was single, I was not, and I believed fervently then that he was the man who would liberate me. Every interaction between us felt furtive, as if we were the only ones who had ever known anything about love or prohibitions against happiness. My breasts were still full of milk during those months; I wondered whether sexy lingerie would be wasted or enhanced by them. I thought of this when he pressed me against the door of our office and kissed my mouth, hand cupping one globe. During my divorce, during that brief affair—I limned meaning from everything I read or listened to. If my lover and I were sitting in the office we shared, he closed the door, and I invested that action with meaning. When he asked an aesthetic question about pornographic images on his computer, I sought meaning. Once, he gave me two mix CDs which I kept and still have. I made two for him. His carried only the dates that he'd burned the disks; mine were cleverly titled. When I listened to the CDs he made me, I imagined our potential lovemaking. Every intimate pronoun became significant. Every genitive case became my marriage. I listened to the music that my longed-for lover arranged for me, sometimes in the car where my husband, who was becoming increasingly paranoid, was passenger. My husband never noticed my newfound interest in music, or if he did I could easily say that a friend of mine had given me the disks, and that she was one of the poets, or whatever. It's easy to lie when you have begun to mistrust and hate your spouse; it's easy to justify things to yourself that you never would have thought justifiable before, especially when he betrayed you first.

3

Song lyrics run the spectrum between clarity and incoherence. Before the Internet, when people owned CDs, tapes, or vinyl albums, the lyrics could be found in the sleeves. These were authorized the way the writers intended them, as opposed to the way they appear on the web: riddled with errors and supported by ads. Kurt Cobain, late Gen-X icon and front man for Nirvana, once complained that Freudian evaluations of his lyrics frustrated him because most of his lyrics were transcribed incorrectly. How many lyrics are perennially misunderstood? One of the more famous misheard lyrics of all time is from "Blinded by the Light," a song written by Bruce Springsteen and covered by Manfred Mann's Earth Band. For many years, along with an inestimable number of other listeners, I heard "wrapped up like a douche," which was supposedly "revved up like a deuce" in the lyrics as the vocalist interpreted them. But this is not the kind of confusion I mean. When we hear lyrics, depending on how closely we listen, we hear verses, and thus poetry. Not everyone interprets lyrics for explication, but it's rare when I choose to ignore lyrics completely and just enjoy a song. More often than not, I'm listening closely, trying to decide if each song I hear creates a balance between sense and sensibility. Music radiates mood and context, but lyrics can offer a work its approximate meaning, insofar as anyone looks for one, and not everyone does. Some writer friends admit to not writing to music with lyrics; others don't write to music at all. Sometimes I can write to music with words if the volume is right; sometimes not. Occasionally, my writing is so engrossing, I write despite any disruption. Sometimes lyrics are enough to distract, sometimes not at all. There is no easy way to prove that lyrics occasionally reach us linguistically, or that they mean anything in isolation that we'll admit to believing.

4

On the CDs my adulterous grad-school lover made for me, one song in particular stood out, as a parable for what I was going through then. Lyrics by Gang of Four added an element of game to feeling like a stranger in one's own home. In punk-laden lines, I heard my lover call my pronominal name through indirection, and then compare the steps that each man might take either forward or backward. My husband and lover, locked in a competition as old as jealousy and desire. "At home she's looking for interest / She says she was ambitious / So she accepts the process." Evenings—when I most feared my husband would discover my secret—made me hesitate to listen overly much to this song. One night after a late class, my lover and I sat terrified across from one another in our shared office, as my two-year-old child pounded on our office door, though the light was off. My husband wandered the halls until he found our toddler, and they went to look for me elsewhere. I dashed down the corridor and made my escape, meeting them guiltily on the ground floor, heart thumping. I do not wish this on anyone: the fear I felt then, my childhood loss of memory, the hopelessness of unrequited love (My lover moved rapidly on after I divorced.) Perhaps this is why I gave up, came to see the love-game of my life for what it is: Forever running down a staircase, shouting things I don't remember, about a loss I cannot understand. I hid my deepest sentiments in certain songs that will always remain difficult to listen to. Whole albums describe my longing in different eras of loss, and become closed to me. Proust's remark that our memories are triggered by smells more than any other sense still holds. Even so, it is in music that I find my memory, and with it, the analogs of pain in covert correspondence.

B-SIDES

"Once there was a way . . ." The family slumbers through yet another golden afternoon. The record skips until someone rights it.

I remember a flag from the funeral I never attended. (Didn't anybody tell her?).

John Lennon died the same year. Something in *Abbey Road,*
the mellow uneasiness of laughter, happiness, and sunlight, lodged
my father on the B-side but it's alright, it's alright . . . that cyclical,
promising word: *if.*

He left his glasses on the bed, the needle on the B-side. My
mom says it was a different album, but I hear *Abbey Road* because I
thought it was written to me. He went outside because the sky and
the wind made everything new again. (Didn't anybody see?)

With albums, it's part intuition where the needle catches, but I
know where to go.

FUGUE YEAR

Author

Why are we in dialogue?

Bach

You needed someone to guide you.

Author

I was drinking absinthe. Does this make you a hallucination?

Bach

Inspiration was imminent else you would not have imagined me.

Author

I'm concerned that I'm losing my mind.

Bach

I cannot know your mind.

Author

What do I know of music? I never learned to play any instrument well enough to understand it.

Bach

You keep notebooks of symmetries. The world is a symmetry.

Author

I like reading about sacred geometry; it is the math and music of Nature. But symmetries of texts and words are not as easily figured with numbers. Music is a pattern of pitch intervals tuned to a pleasurable frequency, presented in perfection of form and time, all numerable. How do I recreate this in words? I would prefer to write what I want, without form and measure.

Bach

I would prefer a clavichord to a piano. But I did not hesitate to try them when offered.

Author

There is so much hubris attached to my mimicry of you. Six years now I've worried over the presumption of modeling your masterpiece.

Bach

Yet you tried.

Author

I could not resist!

Bach

Do you not think I was motivated in much the same way you are, by attempting a great catalogue of my life's work, for the keen student?

Author

But I have not achieved in my forty-some years what you had by the time you were fifty-five, when you began *Die Kunst der Fuge.*

Bach

There is no schedule for when someone should begin.

Author

I feel that I need two decades more to get this right.

Bach

We always ask for more time than we have.

Author
And why you? Why *The Art of Fugue?* Why not an essayist?

Bach
You needed to lay these essays down, to leave them, and be done. You are tired. This is the end of asking the same question.

Author
How can I understand your direction?

Bach
Because you have always loved me, and that love has been a true one.

Author
Wagner's *Ride of the Valkyries* was my first love, on a 45 rpm record, then Tchaikovsky's entire *Nutcracker Suite.* Then you, and your *Well-Tempered Clavier.* You were certainly with me from the time I knew what a record player was, maybe four years old? But then so was Mozart and Beethoven, Duran Duran, Linda Ronstadt, along with all of the LPs my mom and stepdad played: Led Zeppelin, The Beatles, Pink Floyd, David Bowie, Elton John, Aerosmith . . . And then my own LPs: Janet Jackson, Genesis, Peter Gabriel. My cassette tapes: Prince, Madonna, Handel, Sting, R.E.M. My first CDs: Soul II Soul, Gershwin, Strauss, Vivaldi, Saint-Saëns, The Red Hot Chili Peppers, Nirvana, Pearl Jam, Bob Marley, Björk, Lenny Kravitz, Paul Simon, The Master Musicians of Jajouka, Altan . . . After that, the Internet, and too many albums and artists to name. I came up in a time and age of every music I could want. Why you?

Bach
My tempering made the path visible.

Author
I feel like I've been relearning your significance since music theory in high school.

Bach
After abandoning the piano and violin, you had only theory. Such a pity; you enjoyed scales and notation more than playing. You en-

joyed making harmonies with the choir more than singing. Your gift? You were a listener.

Author

I realized my limits.

Bach

You were afraid of a new complexity.

Author

Practicing scales were a pleasure, as were chord progressions. But I couldn't see past them, to a whole that I could comprehend.

Bach

One sees only glimpses.

Author

Here is what I seem to grasp about fugue, from Robert Greenberg's lectures: "What it takes to write a good fugue subject—concision, compactness, and clarity—has to do with the very nature of [the North German composers'] language." If a fugue (a "flight") is a sort of *riff,* that follows the patterns of the human voice, then taking fugue back into a Germanic language like English should be possible, if music and language can be understood as cognates. But then—words cannot be cognates of numbers.

Bach

You must care something for numbers, to obey them so readily. Every essay you have written here is knotted and wound by numbers.

Author

I need the order . . . the seam. I believe utterly that your work is as Greenberg has described it: "a how-to manual, a self-help manual, on how to find what's best in our own imaginations." It is a kind of literature.

Bach

Everything begins with notes.

Author

The words we use are so similar.

Bach

A prelude is an introduction. Suites, canons, and fugues may be meditations or essays. Dances.

Author

Exercises?

Bach

There are only the seven notes of the scale to contend with; best to always be learning.

Author

Stravinsky said as much.

Bach

You have studied your theory but are out of practice.

Author

It all becomes practice.

Bach

As ever it has been.

Author

But I don't want to believe it.

Bach

Your learning has been enough.

Author

I still feel like a failure.

Bach

These things do not resolve. There is never enough time.

Author

You were a collector of books.

Bach

The sacred provides continuous instruction.

Author

But not more than practice? The balance between composing and studying? I can't find it. And somehow we must live between the learning and the creating.

Bach

Creating is as much in the models—the forms—as the fashioning.

Author

How to trust one's self?

Bach

We each begin exactly where we should, with what we have.

Author

When I woke up on that New Year's Day you were sitting by me, bidding me to get up and begin writing to your *Art of Fugue*. Why did this seem reasonable?

Bach

Because you had been afraid and alone. Some of us find solace in our work far too late.

Author

Were you seeking solace when you began *The Art of Fugue?*

Bach

I waited until the end of my life to begin.

Author

You worked on it for a decade.

Bach

A fugue is neither performance, nor execution, but rather a study of flight. A study of freedom in harmony with the order and symmetry of Nature.

Author

You have shown me the strange sides of what had seemed familiar. I am sometimes afraid I have come to the limits of scholarship, too far out of my depth to be an expert.

Bach

I do not wish to taunt you, only to invite you.

Author

I need to unburden myself of all the notes I hear . . . the ones I struggle to interpret.

Bach

You've been reading Hofstadter's tremendous work, where he combines discussions of my *Musical Offering* with those of Escher and Gödel, especially the dialogue, titled "Contracrostipunctus." And you also know Plato's *Phaedrus.* The futility of written words to supplant the beauty and perfection of dialogue and in conversation. This is not a burden but an enlightening.

Author

Hofstadter encourages me. Not only in the way he revives the philosophical dialogue, but also for his insights regarding fugue: "The art of writing a beautiful fugue lies precisely in this ability, to manufacture several different lines, each one of which gives the illusion of having been written for its own beauty, and yet, which when taken together form a whole, which does not feel forced in any way."[5]

Bach

Your friend H. M. suggested that you write in fugues, and W. T. suggested you read *Gödel, Escher, and Bach.* Though this was after you and I began our conversations, you needed the interactions of friends and guides, lest you continue in isolation.

Author

I thank each of them, and I did join myself to *The Art of Fugue,* as you asked. Hofstadter describes *The Musical Offering* as a "fugue of fugues." He says that "it is an intellectual construction which reminds [him] in ways [he] cannot express of the beautiful many-voiced fugue of the human mind."[6]

Bach

Are you surprised, then, that *The Musical Offering* did not attract you?

Author

I am far more interested in the "many-voiced fugue" of the human heart. Though the *Offering* was a gift to a king, I see *The Art of Fugue* as a gift you made to yourself. It was your love of fugue that guided you. I hope my perspective is not seen as an appropriation.

Bach

This is the way art proceeds: as a series of abductions.

Author

It seems like that's a quote, but I can't recall whose.

Bach

You are obsessed with possessing things that cannot be owned, of knowing the source of everything. As soon as you let go of that need, your life's meaning will open up to you. That is what really happened when I encoded my own name in the final fugue. I realized I wanted it to remain incomplete, entirely my own, left open for others to finish. It would have been the same, had I written the rest of the fugue on a final page and then lit it on fire!

Author

This would make Indra Hughes's 2007 dissertation correct.[7]

Bach

What does it matter? The question is still open.

Author

What question?

Bach

Whether the work can ever be finished. My experience has been that we sooner exhaust our medium than we find the end of what speaks to us through it.

Author

Is your remark intended to make me feel better or worse about this project?

Bach

Better, most certainly.

Author

But this means that I'll eventually run out of prose forms, or find the limits of my knowledge of them.

Bach

Just as you will assuredly run out of fugues in my *Art of Fugue,* and still there are those who will complete what you left open, unfinished. This is a gesture toward incompleteness, and further, toward the utter inexhaustibility stretching beyond all earthly things. The piano surpassed the harpsichord, yet pianos rot in time. Paper disintegrates or is burnt and blown away, but the work remains to be done. After my death, Leipzig meat cutters wrapped their butchery in the pages of my abandoned compositions. My music was worth less than the paper it was scripted on. Such is the way of all things.

Author

You still haven't told me why *you* came to me and not someone else in your place.

Bach

Because you have always loved me, unceasing.

Author

Is that enough? I've never known you in any way but through your music, and even that remains only a partial understanding.

Bach

There is no partial understanding between us. You love me as you love writing, and all art, all music. You practice only what you love, and to practice, you must study intently enough to emulate movements and measures. When you count the measures of my fugues and canons, and then count your own paragraphs, words, and characters, you are showing your love for what you certainly understand. You are simply counting the things that you love, not limiting them, or seeking to be comprehensive. One person is not comprehensive, though two opposites might be.

Author

Now you're beginning to sound like those Zen koans that Hofstadter writes about.

Bach

You have known about my passion for riddles all along.

Author

I still lack the confidence to believe that what I am doing is worthwhile, or that I interpret or understand your work correctly.

Bach

My son was more renowned than I was during my own lifetime, and yet I left him with a puzzle he could not unlock. Inexhaustible and incomplete, as are all the works of man.

Author

My mortality is ever in the front of my mind.

Bach

We are granted only an instant to hear the notes, then are asked to play them back.

Author

How then is anything that we attempt in life significant? If I will not ever reach the end of prose, if it will always remain some mystery for the working out?

Bach

The question lives because it cannot be answered. You live because you do not stop. You continue to live, that is all.

Author

So how does it all end?

Bach

First you must write it.

Author

And the canons?

Bach

Your rests.

Author

They overrun their course sometimes. I am reminded of Glenn Gould's remark in "Anatomy of Fugue" on *Festival Presents*: "The great writers of canon always know when to quit." I'm afraid I'm locked into dialogue with you and I don't know my way out.

Bach

Fugues should seem freer in contrast.

Author

You are not offended that I attempt what you did perfectly, so many years before?

Bach

Yours is the lot of the living.

Author

That's a grim way of saying I have no choice.

Bach

I cannot prevent you from trying.[8]

Author

Perhaps you are here so that I don't embarrass myself?

Bach

Allow your soul its own fearless counting.

Author

Perhaps there's a point in saying goodbye to our muses, lest we draw attention to their ultimate inaccessibility . . .

FRAGMENTS TOWARD
AN INDEX OF BIRDS

&

"(What's Your) Angle," G
"11:11," S
"50 Pieces," T

A concordance is an essay with no discernible pronouns. It is an anonymous parable wherein the writer retreats to the quiet of index. Dictionaries, lists (all abecedarian collections) record patterns that lead the writer on. One day it all becomes a living thing. The unfinished words queue to be counted: anemone, atmosphere, breather, calcium, columns, crash, desert, disaster, fades, fall (-en, -ing, -s), fatal, fingerlings, fire (-s), gaze, glass, hollow, home, horse (-s), kittens, light, listen, machine, moon, muddy, name, nothing, oh no, parchment, rain (-s), salsify, shell, snack (-s), spheres, spores, tenuous, thistles, vagaries, valley (-ies), whiskey, window.

A

A. See *Armchair Apocrypha*
A1, "Fiery Crash," A
A2, "Imitosis," A

A3, "Plasticities," A
A4, "Heretics," A
A5, "Armchairs," A
A6, "Dark Matter," A
A9, "Cataracts," A
A10, "Scythian Empires," A
A11, "Spare-ohs," A

"Action/Adventure," W

alone, *by one's self*
    A2: be there alone
    B11: be there alone
    B13: stop bleeding alone
    M5: are walking alone
    N17: you're not alone
    N4: too much time alone
    P13: they're not alone
    P7: standing all alone
    R15: be there alone
    S10: I'm all alone now
    T6: I'm all alone
    W2: we're basically alone
    W3: being alone

Andrew Bird & The Mysterious Production of Eggs (2005) Righteous
    Babe. *See also under* P—P14

"Anonanimal," N

apropos, *appropriate to the moment*
    A1: to say something apropos

arc, -s, *electric discharge*
    B9: till the arc spits
    R3: the arcs spit

"Arcs and Coulombs," R, *cf.* "Lusitania," B

Armchair Apocrypha (2007) Fat Possum. *See also under* A–A11

"Armchairs," A

B

B. See *Break It Yourself*
B1, "Desperation Breeds . . . ," B
B3, "Danse Caribe," B
B4, "Give It Away," B
B5, "Eyeoneye," B
B6, "Lazy Projector," B
B7, "Near Death Experience Experience," B
B9, "Lusitania," B
B10, "Orpheo Looks Back," B
B11, "Sifters," B
B12, "Fatal Shore," B
B13, "Hole in the Ocean Floor," B
"Banking on a Myth," P

bereft, *without something, often an immaterial lack*
    P3: till you're bereft
    S7: forlorn and bereft
    S13: bereft of fire

"Beware," G
"Beyond the Valley of Three White Horses," H

bird, *a winged, egg-laying creature usually capable of flight*
    A11: small flightless birds
    G13: a bird's nest
    N13: birds will sing
    P9: macramé bird of prey

blackbird, *a bird of mostly black plumage*
    O1: name is a blackbird

Break It Yourself (2011) Mom & Pop. *See also under* B–B13

A concordance is the aesthetic product of frequency. No one writes it. This concordance is nine feet long. Bird's "oh no" can be one word and also "weather systems." Or, Chicago, and how it felt to be alone. ("If you promise spring then I know you are a liar" [N13]). The weather radio bleated warnings and years later, in Tennessee, tornadoes skated along the sides of mountains like they were never supposed to do. "Perhaps you can write your way out of it" became pronouns and referents, then choices, unfurling.

break, **-ing**, *to separate, often forcibly; forcefully coming apart*
    A1: starting to break up
    B5: break your heart; break it yourself
    B6: breaking up at all
    M9: heart may break

breeding, *procreating, proliferating*
    A1: breeding superstition
    B1: we keep breeding desperation
    H1: desperation that we're breeding

burrow, *to nestle, to tunnel to make a home*
    N2: burrow into me

C

"Candy Shop," G

cartographer, *one who creates maps*
    A5: I was a cartographer

"Case in Point," S
"Cataracts," A

ciphers, *secret encoded messages*
    O1: the serifs and ciphers

cloud, **-s**, *suspended particles at a high altitude*
    B3: mistaking clouds for mountains

H5: clouds we keep on seeding
W8: another cloud begins

"Cock o' the Walk," T

code, *system of symbols for transmitting secret messages*
   N8: I crack the codes

Songwriter Andrew Bird often articulates the whimsy, gravity, absurdity, and richness of human experience by remaining "more interested in feel, than in exact, specific definitions." There's a narrative glimpse, but not enough to build a story. Bird uses words as another kind of instrument and once explained to interviewer Melissa Block that writing melodies preceded the lyrics: "If one thing is fixed and then the words have to conform to the fixed melodies, then it's like cracking codes." Working within form becomes a way of finding the hidden language underneath.

"Confession, The" G, *cf.* "Privateers, The" N
"Core and Rind," S

crooked bow, *a bow that is not straight or even*
   A5: time it's a crooked bow : : time's a crooked bow
   B6: time's a crooked bow

D

"Danse Caribe," B
"Dark Matter," A
"Dear Old Greenland," S

desperation, *near hopelessness*
   B1: we keep breeding desperation : : instead of breeding desperation
   H1: it's not desperation

"Desperation Breeds . . . ," B
"Dora Goes to Town," G

doubt, **-s**, *a lack of surety*
    B12: never know any doubt
    S5: these few doubts disserve me

"Drinking Song in the Grande Style, A" G

drown, **-ed**, *submersion which can lead to death*
    M5: watched her drown : : why have you drowned me?
    O3: drowned in her own curls

E

"Effigy," N

effigy, *imitation or likeness*
    N4: when you long to burn this effigy

encrypted, *encoded*
    N8: encrypted numbers on bathroom stalls

In the commentary for "Trimmed and Burning: Live at the Orange Peel, Asheville, NC, September 12, 2007," Bird attributes the origin of "Capsized" to exploration of an old blues tune. Aside from the Orange Peel being the last place the author saw Bird perform, this date was the author's birthday, and one celebrated in Chicago most likely, far from home. The first listen comes almost a decade later, on a dreary January day becoming darker. The continuity of a songwriter's work is like that of any other kind of writer.

"Eugene," T
"Eyeoneye," B

F

"Fake Palindromes," P
"Fatal Shore," B

feathers, *the light appendages growing from a bird's skin*
    O1: feathers are warm in molasses
    T11: I can puff up my feathers

"Feetlips," G
"Fiery Crash," A
"Fitz and the Dizzy Spells," N

finches, *small birds*
    A11: the finches and sparrows build nests

G

G. See *Oh! The Grandeur*
G1, "Candy Shop," G
G2, "Tea and Thorazine," G
G3, "Wishing for Contentment," G
G5, "The Idiot's Genius," G
G6, "Vidalia," G
G7, "Beware," G
G8, "Dora Goes to Town," G
G9, "Feetlips," G
G13, "(What's Your) Angle," G
G14, "The Confession," G
G15, "A Drinking Song in the Grande Style," G

game, *play, contest, or amusement*
    G1: of this silly game
    P5: we'll play a new game
    P6: the game is rigged
    P11: running for the game

"Give It Away," B
"Glass Figurine," T
"Gris-Gris," T

H

H. See *Hands of Glory*
H1, "Three White Horses," H
H5, "Something Biblical," H
H7, "Orpheo," H
H8, "Beyond the Valley of Three White Horses," H

Hands of Glory (2012) Mom + Pop Music. *See also under* H–H8

"Happy Birthday, The" P
"Heretics," A
"Hole in the Ocean Floor," B
"How Indiscreet," S

I

I. See *I Want to See Pulaski at Night*
I4, "Pulaski at Night," I

"I," W, *cf.* "Imitosis," A

I Want to See Pulaski at Night (2013) Grimsey Records. *See also under*
    I–I4

"Ides of Swing," T
"Idiot's Genius, The" G
"Imitosis," A, *cf.* "I," W

L

"Lazy Projector," B

lost, *cannot be recovered or found*
    M9: eternally lost love

N4: of a man who has lost his way
N10: the troglodytes lost their sight
P6: when the words we use have lost their bite
S1: will all be lost if you let it in
S7: lost his way going to town
T10: this song's like a lost ship at sea

love, *intense affection*
A5: learn to love
B4: your love was a commodity
B10: where love turns to love turns to fear
H7: where love turns to fear
M9: eternally lost love
N5: love of hate acts as an axis
N10: I love this song
N17: you dream of the kind of love you knew the day you're born
P6: talent, genius, love
P9: And love, oh, love : : is my, love is
T2: When you make love to whomever you please

Friends turn to a listener who nods at their betrayal and the broken-ness, after trying to become a replacement lover and failing. ("Why do some show no mercy, while others are painfully shy?" [A2]). Words stick in one's throat most of the time, except when quoting others. A constancy of purpose can entertain. "Work is the great consolation," Jean-Léon Gérôme often remarked. For now, something written, and for another time, a lover: echoes of some passion or another. Romance languishes unsustained by the ego. Submission to form frees the heart.

lover, *one who loves or is loved, usually romantically*
N13: still my lover won't return to me
N15: section 8 city lover

An essay is rarely what one actually wants. It is the lover who be-comes the momentary mnemonic. The shape that lyric makes in the evening is different from a song in the morning. Abandoned words are remembered as a constraint. If this writing is a corset, unlace the top two tiers and contemplate an exciting finish. If the eyelets seem too narrow, then someone is in a hurry. Would that there were only a concordance here, because no one reads a reference end-to-end unless grasping at the entirety of loss.

"Lull," W
"Lusitania," B, *cf.* "Arcs and Coulombs," R

M

M. See *Music of Hair*
M5, "Two Sisters," M
M9, "Pathetique," M
M10, "Song of Foot," M

man, *male human being*
> N2: for inside me grows a man
> N4: like the words of a man who's spent a little too much time alone
> O1: this is a story man
> S7: oh man anything to get away from this shame
> S13: I shall return a different man
> T1: thin-skinned man
> T6: old man in the overalls
> T11: be the old man at this here scene

master, *one who dominates or controls, or an artist of highest skill*
> B6: who owns the master
> N2: feeding from the arms of the master
> P6: and when his master plan is unfurled

"Masterfade," P
"Masterswarm," N

measure, -d, *quantify, quantified*
> P5: we'll measure your brain
> P7: they'll have to measure in tons

T6: find your measured paces

"Measuring Cups," P

melody, *notes in a distinctive sequence or pleasurable arrangement*
   B11: biggest melody you've never heard before
   R15: biggest melody you've never heard before

memory, *faculty of remembering*
   B6: if memory serves us
   O1: this is a story about the memory of water
   P10: in the memory of a garbage can

Bending Genre opens randomly to Mary Cappello's "Propositions; Provocations; Inventions" and a circled passage: "Coincidence and available prescience always helps me along, and in the course of my writing, I found myself within earshot of one of Bach's famous 'two-part inventions.'" Cappello asks, "Could language do what this music for piano was capable of?" The page had been read and marked two years ago. If only readers had an internal, perfect concordance of all that they had read. Knowing how many times one has crossed Bach in a year, perhaps.

mind, *the center of one's thoughts and feelings*
   A5: it didn't cross your mind at all
   G3: a nauseous elation comes to mind
   G7: just keep in mind
   G14: you call it peace of mind
   M10: my mind doesn't have my best interests in mind
   N12: you call it peace of mind
   S1: it puts my mind in traction
   S2: you don't know my mind
   S13: all the disparate fragments of my mind

"Minor Stab," T

Music of Hair (1996) Grimsey Records. *See also under* M–M10

"MX Missiles," P

myth, *stories mortals tell about the divine in order to feel meaningful
      and relevant*
>   P6: taking all our myths to the bank

N

N. See *Noble Beast*
N1, "Oh No," N
N2, "Masterswarm," N
N3, "Fitz and the Dizzy Spells," N
N4, "Effigy," N
N5, "Tenuousness," N
N6, "Nomenclature," N
N8, "Not a Robot, But a Ghost," N
N10, "Anonanimal," N
N11, "Natural Disaster," N
N12, "The Privateers," N
N13, "Souverian," N
N15, "Section 8 City," N
N17, "Take Courage," N

"Naming of Things, The" P
"Natural Disaster," N
"Near Death Experience Experience," B
"Nervous Tic Motion of the Head to the Left, A" P

never, *speculation of future absence and lack of being*
>   B4: I swore I'd never take anyone there again
>   B11: you never heard before
>   B12: if you never knew us
>   G7: never with a thought
>   I4: it never looks right
>   N13: you'll never fear anymore
>   O2: there was never reason to worry
>   O3: that never seemed to end
>   R15: you never heard before
>   S1: I'll never ever feel it again
>   S8: never the twain shall meet

T10: though I've never been
W3: the sun's never shone

The Oxford English Dictionary is a sort of time-focused concordance. Words were compiled on the basis of their appearance in *what* text and in *which* year. The shifts in meaning were noted, and no doubt the paper in that office would have been lengthy had it been taped end-to-end. Writers of indexes and abecedarian prose often edit with physical pages, scissors, and tape. Years ago, a friend of essayist M. Disler would have entered an editor's workshop when the Bond Alphabet was in production. Admiration brings this memory, and others.

"Night Sky," R. *See also* "Sifters," B

night, *cyclical period of global darkness created by the earth's rotation*
    B6: every day the night must fall
    B11: what if I were the night sky
    I4: Pulaski at night
    M5: wolves by night and sun by day
    N17: night's falling
    P4: some lonely night we can get together
    R15: if I were the night sky
    S1: I've been driving all night
    S10: last night
    S12: I saw you last night
    T11: Pulaski at night
    T12: wait for night fall

Noble Beast (2009) Fat Possum. *See also under* N—N17

nomenclature, *set of language signs operating as a vocabulary of names*
    N6: could you bring a different nomenclature : : our nomencla-
        ture is washing away

An indexer codifies information, interacting with the form and content of prose. Like a page designer, the author of a concordance, dictionary, or atlas will chart the placement of bold and italic text.

Definitions and explanatory images appear regularly. Structure is reinforced by attention to form and thoroughness is measured by the encoded value of collected information. Ability to access the information and decipher the code is expected of the reader, but processing cannot be too complex. A referential text illuminates correspondences and patterns. It fails if it is opaque.

"Nomenclature," N

Norman (Original Motion Picture Soundtrack) (2011) Mom + Pop Music. *See also under* R–R15

"Not a Robot, But a Ghost," N

numerology, *systems by which numbers are meaningful articulators of qualitative experience*
   N5: for those who live and die from numerology

Neuroticisms of obsession and compulsion aside, counting can become an addiction. Blue seventy-eight, echo eighty-four, then seventy-two, one hundred and thirty-eight. This concordance is ninety, followed by seventy-nine magpies, engine sixty-one, a tense one hundred and eighty-eight, and solo, one-hundred and thirty. The circle is completed by one hundred and twenty-two tritones. One hundred and eighty-four mirrors interview seventy-one. This sentence brings this paragraph to sixty-seven words. A paradox is created when a number becomes a word and that word is counted. Meter counts in the measure of universal time.

"Nuthinduan Waltz," T

O

O. See *Soldier On*
O1, "The Trees Were Mistaken," O
O2, "Sic of Elephants," O
O3, "The Water Jet Cilice," O

ocean, **-s**, *great bodies of water that dress the earth, responsible for atmosphere and life*

B11: sound is a wave like a wave on the ocean : : moon plays the
    ocean like a violin
  B13: there's a hole in the ocean floor
  H5: oceans of plasma
  N3: cliffs to the ocean
  R15: sound is a wave like a wave on the ocean : : moon plays the
    ocean like a violin

"Oh No," N

Oh! The Grandeur (1999) Rykodisc. *See also under* G–G15

"Opposite Day," P
"Orpheo Looks Back," B. *See also* "Orpheo," H
"Orpheo," H. *See also* "Orpheo Looks Back," B

P

P. See *Andrew Bird & The Mysterious Production of Eggs*
P2, "Sovay," P
P3, "A Nervous Tic Motion of the Head to the Left," P
P4, "Fake Palindromes," P
P5, "Measuring Cups," P
P6, "Banking on a Myth," P
P7, "Masterfade," P
P8, "Opposite Day," P
P9, "Skin Is, My," P
P10, "The Naming of Things," P
P11, "MX Missiles," P
P13, "Tables and Chair," P
P14, "The Happy Birthday," P

palindromes, *anagram created by mirroring one sequence against itself*
  A2: with his machinations and his palindromes

P4: "Fake Palindromes"
W2: with our machinations and palindromes

To have been a palindrome of another is to always see palindromes and be attracted to them. "Fake Palindromes" leads the curious into an entire album. An album becomes a discovery. One day there is no shortage of songs and the wafting metaphors, words, melodies. One day it all becomes violin ("The moon plays the ocean like a violin." [B11; R15]). Another evening, a whistle in a park invokes the remembered tune. The hollowed lips speak into hallowed space, an embarrassingly lateral, semantic glissando. It is Chicago, 2007, or thereabouts.

"Pathetique," M
"Privateers, The" N, *cf.* "Confession, The" G
"Plasticities," A
"Pulaski at Night," I

R

R. See *Norman (Original Motion Picture Soundtrack)*
R3, "Arcs and Coulombs," R
R15, "Night Sky," R

S

S. See *The Swimming Hour*
S1, "Two Way Action," S
S2, "Core and Rind," S
S3, "Why," S
S4, "11:11," S
S5, "Case in Point," S
S7, "Way Out West," S
S8, "Waiting to Talk," S
S10, "Satisfied," S
S11, "Headsoak," S

S12, "How Indiscreet," S
S13, "Dear Old Greenland," S

"Satisfied," S
"Scythian Empires," A
"Section 8 City," N

self, *the imagined perspective one has apart from everything else in the
    world*
    A6: do you wonder where the self resides
    G2: consummate a self-pleasing artificiality
    O3: tales of ritual self-torture
    S12: your self-destruction is so complete
    W3: I'm rambling on rather self-consciously

Andrew Bird's 2012 performance at The Tabernacle in Atlanta drew
this listener into live music, and deeper into the mystery of performance in general. What does it mean to perform an index? And how
does a writer perform a fugue? TJ Dawe's online essay "The Fugue
Fugue" explains using Andrew Bird's looping technique as one of
many examples: "He'll lay out a single line on the violin, and loop
it. Then play a second track over that, and loop that, and a third
track, and a fourth, and so on."

shore, *the place where the fluid laps and sometimes the edge of what's
    familiar*
    B9: you're laying mines along the shore
    B11: pushing and pulling from shore to shore
    B12: on a fatal shore : : when are you coming to shore
    N13: we will meet on a fatal shore
    P2: then a word washed to shore
    R15: pushing and pulling from shore to shore

Dawe elaborates: "And he sings. And sometimes plays guitar. And
whistles. And plays the xylophone, in tandem with his whistles.
Looping anything he wants to use. Building on anything he wants
to build on." Dawe extends his own fugue: "Andrew Bird never repeats the way he performs a song. He won't change it so much that

it's unrecognizable, but he'll never play it exactly like it is on the
album. Or the way he played it the night before. Every performance
is a variation. Every song sets up myriad possibilities."

"Sic of Elephants," O
"Sifters," B. *See also* "Night Sky," R
"Skin Is, My," P

sing, **-s**, *a function, often of the human voice, to render beautiful and
    meaningful sound*
    A4: so sing a song about it
    A5: the song that silence sings
    B1: beekeeper sing of your frustration
    M10: my feet, they speak and sing
    N13: the thrushes sing
    P14: sing a birthday / sing it like it's going to be your last day
    P9: to come down and sing
    T2: bounce and sing

Soldier On (2007) Grimsey Records, Fargo Records. *See also under*
    O–O3

"Something Biblical," H
"Song of Foot," M
"Souverian," N
"Sovay," P
"Spare-ohs," A

sparrows, *small birds*
    A11: the finches and sparrows build nests
    B3: the thing that brings the sparrows to the fountains

story, *a way of organizing and relating experience*
    I4: I write you a story
    M5: the strings that would have her story sung
    O1: this is a story : : some kind of a story
    P5: just another children's story
    S2: I tell you a story

In a beautiful essay titled "Adventures in the Reference Section," Kevin Haworth writes: "Lists lead to narrative. Information leads to imagination." He writes that "reference books are inherently hybrid. They mix text and image, numbers and letters. They assert authority while hiding the authorial voice behind the editorial board, the anonymously written article." He ends with an extended blessing of gratitude: "Thank you for the OED, the story of our language masquerading as a dictionary. Thank you for the abstract and the annotated bibliography and the footnote and the endnote."

Swimming Hour, The (2001) Rykodisc. *See also under* S–S13

T

T. See *Thrills*
T1, "Minor Stab," T
T2, "Ides of Swing," T
T3, "Glass Figurine," T
T6, "50 Pieces," T
T9, "Eugene," T
T10, "Gris-Gris," T
T11, "Cock o' the Walk," T
T12, "Nuthinduan Waltz," T

"Tables and Chair," P
"Take Courage," N
"Tea and Thorazine," G

tense, *a condition a verb takes to indicate time*
     N12: speak of me in the present tense

"Tenuousness," N

thought, *a function of the mind*
     A6: and does the thought of all this red and black : : thought of
          tongues that taste you back
     A11: I just thought I was a kind of bird
     G7: never with a thought to dare

G9: you thought Somepeople was a tragic name
M5: he thought there must be something to these bones
N1: of what was thought but unsaid
P7: I thought at last I'd found a situation you can't explain
P11: I thought you were a life-sized paper doll
S1: you wouldn't ordinarily have thought of
S2: what you thought was the core
S3: I thought that time would tell
T3: the thought of you makes me sanguine
T6: I thought perhaps we could sit down for tea
W4: that's when I thought I'd be the cross in your t

"Three White Horses," H

Thrills (1998) Rykodisc. *See also under* T–T12

time, *a measure of existence used by human beings*
A5: time it's a crooked bow : : oh time's a crooked bow : : in time
    you need to learn to love
B11: at the same time
B5: all this time it took
B6: time's a crooked bow
G2: time in a mental institution
G6: there was a time
G7: in time you find so few
G8: you heard me the first time
G14: your one time offer
M10: it's a proper time
M9: for a long time
N12: your one time offer
N4: too much time alone
N6: it's time we ask the sea
N8: time strips the gears till you forget what they were for
P2: this time
P9: there's time spent
R15: born at the same time
S3: I thought that time would tell
S5: time to face the nation
T6: a long, long time

W4: I'm wasting your time
W8: every time we turn the soil

The page is a field into which expression enters. Artists regularly ex-
periment with position and context. Nothing is more provocative
than the playfulness of structure. Margot Singer, in her essay "On
Scaffolding, Hermit Crabs, and the Real False Document" writes
that poets build rooms whereas writers of prose "tend to think of
structure in terms of time, not space." Her ultimate conclusion is
that "use of 'found form' in creative nonfiction reminds us that the
literary text is always a construction, not a transparent window onto
'reality' or the 'truth.'"[9]

"Trees Were Mistaken, The" O
"Two Sisters," M
"Two Way Action," S

                              V

"Vidalia," G

                              W

W. See *Weather Systems*
W2, "I," W
W3, "Lull," W
W4, "Action/Adventure," W
W7, "Weather Systems," W

"Waiting to Talk," S

wandering, *often directionless movement*
    T10: this song's like a lost ship at sea that's the same as wandering

"Water Jet Cilice, The" O
"Way Out West," S

Weather Systems (2003) Righteous Babe. *See also under* W–W7

weather systems, *complex of atmospheric conditions*
  G9: his weather systems tempered and tame
  P6: a handsome bid on the weather systems of the world
  W8: I can see weather systems of the world

"Weather Systems," W
"Why," S
"Wishing for Contentment," G

woman, *female human being*
  M5: one old woman was walking alone
  S4: I once knew a woman

Y

Memory is checked by research and relieved by verification. In 1966, Yoko Ono exhibited her "Ceiling Painting" at the Indica Gallery of London. A white ladder enticed viewers to a framed area of the ceiling where a hand lens hung which would allow viewers to read one word in miniscule lettering. John Lennon saw the work and was drawn to Ono, marrying her three years later. Lennon in retrospect remarked, "I would have been quite disappointed if it had said 'NO,' but was saved by the fact it said 'YES.'"

yes, *affirmation*
  B3: anything but my yes and no
  G1: yes to your glamour : : yes little mama
  G13: it keeps things curious yes
  G8: yes sir
  P8: yes it took me by surprise
  S12: yes she's gone down fast
  S8: yes it seems that everyone's just waiting to talk
  T10: yes those southern cats
  T2: yes you're dreaming

MUSES AND MAGPIES

A Personal History of Lyrical Analysis, Delusion, and Certain Social Networks

My mentor once referenced a line that has always stayed in my memory. Like most of his best quips, this particular one changed over time the more I thought about it, until I finally looked it up. In the poem "Lillian Harvey," Gerald Stern describes the obsessive love of composer Charles Koechlin for the actress, Lillian Harvey. This poem reaches anyone who knows what it is like to idolize an individual far past the possibility of a real encounter. Although I remembered my teacher paraphrasing the line into advice ("You can't fuck the muse"), the poem actually admonishes that "You never fuck the muse." Same difference, really, except by reading the poem now I find such sadness there in the story that belies the wit. Koechlin composed music for Harvey, who was at first flattered but then later uncomfortable once she realized his unhealthy affection for her. He worshipped her to the point of his own suffering. My thoughts about muses have frequently run back to this idea, of their painful inaccessibility to the artist, and also, how any idealized love diminishes in the bright light of day. But I also think about the magic of inspiration and creativity, how like love it is, and how when we feel ourselves to be in love, we are in that same heightened and sensual state, ready to make meaning of anything at all.

Xanadu, the 80s film (with the great soundtrack) starring Olivia Newton-John, portrayed the direct influence of the Muses in the lives of artists. Having been a young girl when the movie premiered,

I was captivated by the idea of special angels whose job it was to inspire artistic creation. The Muses are the origin for our words "music" and also "museum," which is the place where they are worshipped. We say that we "muse" over ideas when we study them. The three elder Boetian Muses were Aoede, muse of song; Melete, the muse of practice, thought, or meditation; and Mnema, the muse of memory. Later the three were expanded to nine total, and said to be the children of Zeus and Mnemosyne, and these are the ones we are most familiar with.

In Ovid's *Metamorphoses,* the nine Muses were challenged by the nine daughters of King Pierus to a singing contest. King Pierus bragged on his daughters (the Pierides) and puffed up their egos, leading them to believe that competing with the Muses was a good idea. The Muses sang the story of Persephone who was kidnapped by an amorous Hades and taken to the Underworld. The Pierides, on the other hand, blasphemed the gods, mocked the Muses even after losing, and thus were transformed into magpies. This always struck me as one of the fairer transformational punishments in Ovid's telling, because the Pierides were, as a result of their hubris, condemned to cawing in imitation of the Muses. This, like no other story I know, makes a strong argument for invoking the Muses at the beginning of any great work, else be cursed to imitate (badly) whatever art their patronage could have inspired otherwise.

Lest this moment be lost to connect to other mythological emblems of music, Orpheus, if you recall, was the best of poets and musicians until his wife Eurydice was bitten by a snake on their wedding day. He traveled to Hades to plead for her life, and permission was granted because Persephone intervened on his behalf with Hades. Still, Orpheus lost her forever because he looked back in disbelief at Eurydice as they were leaving the Underworld. Andrew Bird illustrates the moment and the setting beautifully in "Orpheo Looks Back": "You must cross the muddy river / Where love turns to fear." The condition that Hades placed on Orpheus was rooted in the inevitability that doubt will contaminate even the most immortal of loves, and that Orpheus would fail to keep walking forward trusting that his love (still a shade) was walking with him.

Because of Orpheus's prominence as the mythological *human* figure we most associate with music, it's not surprising that there are numerous songs about him and the story of his tragic love. *Hadestown,* a folk opera featuring the talents of Anaïs Mitchell, Justin Vernon (of Bon Iver), and Ani DiFranco (among others), tells the entire story of Orpheus and Eurydice. The critical moment when Eurydice is lost comes through the song "Doubt Comes In," when we are told it comes in with "tricky fingers," that it comes in with "fickle tongues." The story of the tragic pair always fascinated me, because in so many ways it captures the ascendancy of death over all earthly beings. Romantic love, so centered in the flesh, is a part of that deep mortal cycle of birth and decay, and yet it is also love which empowers the being to bring light from the darkness and to create beauty capable of transcending all time. The Muses are said to have gathered up the shattered body of Orpheus and buried him, which deepens the cyclical well of story and song that is myth.

Myth frequently undergirds the way I see the world, and it is no accident that theories of psychology use mythological characters to describe the character types we see in the world. Oedipus, Electra, and Narcissus represent complexes that any one of us might fall into or fall in love with. And so it is that Orpheus is the perfect image of the damaged artist, the musician who fills the quiet of loss with harmonies of either delight or sorrow; Orpheus is brutally dismembered by his most zealous fans, the Bacchantes, because he won't sleep with them. Whenever musicians are stalked or pawed by groupies, or their work is exploited or undersold, I remember Orpheus. My mind is ever on the ways music drives us into madness, or relieves the same, depending on who inspires it and what they sing. That music and madness and obsession could be so linked, I find significant, but such is the way of deep myth.

∴ ∴

As I am prone to find meaning in all things, I've been deeply superstitious of omens, augers, and synchronicities my entire life. Some signs come to me in music. For a long time after I fell in love again, all of my signs were songs. For nearly four months, I neurotically maintained a notebook which chronicled the signs of what I had taken to mean more than just songs, or the patterns of habit amid the seeming randomness. Over the years I had become suspicious of my attractions, and acknowledged that whatever love I imagined I wanted might not be best for me. I based this concern on the fortune cookie message that I received soon after I had begun my new job: "Make sure the love that you seek / is the love that you need." I taped the slip of paper over my sink so that I could stare at it every morning when I washed my dishes. Never mind that love and obsession had never been clearly separate for me. But I fell in love again, for the first time in years. There were complications from the outset. The situation was less than ideal. We were not in a position to date one another, even if we *did* share feelings of attraction, though I'm not sure if we ever did. We settled on fast friendship in an unspoken way, and realized we shared a mutual love of music. After a late evening with friends at a local bar, he sent me an invitation to a music-sharing social network.

The network interface was simple. The playlists the user created were on the left side. The center represented an active screen, showing the playlists that were being played or viewed at that moment. On the right side was the area reserved for friends' listening activity. The top portion of the right side displayed "Favorites," people selected by you to follow closely, and the bottom portion was an active feed, showing what music was being played by all of the people the user knew on a social network who also used the music service, as long as they had chosen to make the songs they played publicly viewable. Every user chose whether or not to play music publicly or privately, and data about music that one played publicly (or *socially*) could be seen. Listening data could also be sent to the main social network, which continually spewed information updates on the right hand side of its screen.

The music database was searchable, and as of June 2015, the service had more than 75 million active users. All users, even those who listened for free, could listen to any song, album, or artist without having to listen to several "similar" songs. With this service I could have near-limitless access to music from all over the world. Within a month of joining, my habits became altered. Although at the time I coordinated the journalism program in the English department, I stopped caring about the news, and ceased listening to NPR on my way to and from campus. Instead, I made playlists of new music that I enjoyed and played them everywhere I went. Every day I found new music, musicians, or albums I'd never heard before. In hindsight, my subscription to the service was a profoundly frugal investment, since I didn't have to buy music in order to enjoy it. I created so many playlists, a social network friend mentioned that he "couldn't find the shallow end" of my playlists and instead "took up his towel and went home." Afterward, I felt self-conscious about how much time I was spending listening to music publicly.

At the time I subscribed to the music service, there was no way to unlink it from my most frequently used social media account. In the past I had disconnected from social media in order to concentrate on my work during busy times, but I could no longer do this without losing my access to all the music I wanted. Tom Waits growls in a song from the folk opera *The Black Rider,* and speaks directly to me, it seems: "Kid: you're hooked / Heavy as lead."

Both networks thrived as a result of the users' own voluntary involvement. What compelled me to mindlessly scroll social media when I should have been working was the same force that compelled me to listen to songs openly so that my friends could see them, or publish dozens of playlists. I quickly formed an addiction to music, and considered it healthier than my other vices, such as overeating. I began to lose weight and lose sleep, as I couldn't pull myself away from music for anything less important than a house fire.

At first, I openly played songs I'd picked up from friends until I began to feel uncomfortable listening to the music someone else liked in front of everyone else I knew. That was my first insight into the ways our listening habits betray us. What's more, I began to ravenously desire more music, and more friends to share it with. With only two to begin with—my closest female confidant and my secret crush—things rapidly became complicated. Already I had noticed that someone who listened to an album within the same two or three days of someone else would be "outed" by social media to all of their mutual friends. Two people might both listen to Neil Young at the same time and social media would report it from the data supplied by the music sharing service. Granted, one could turn off publicizing one's listening habits, but the temptation to make one's self known to others in a particular way was what kept social networks operative. We wanted some people, but not all, to know that we liked what they liked, or that we had something to say about their interests. That is primarily what human beings communicate to each other publicly, in mixed company. Most social media was nothing if not mixed company. Unsurprisingly, when a relationship is secret, uncertain, and/or inappropriate, most people will find an alternative medium for communication, and they sometimes imagined social networks to be that alternative, never thinking that others could see and make inferences, based on online behavior. I discovered it was possible to develop camaraderie simply by liking someone's music, by choosing to broadcast to the world that I liked listening to this or that song openly, especially at the same time as another person listened. The feeling was extraordinary, to listen to a piece of music with someone else, at the same time, publicly, yet privately, alone in my own home. The ability to draw particular friends on the social network into a tighter circle was what I liked best about the service. For a time, I was what some researchers might call a "power-user."

According to a research study done in February 2012, a "power-user" was a part of the 20–30% of users who were active on a weekly or daily basis as opposed to infrequent use over the course of a month. Given that a single so-called power-user had the potential to affect up to eight million people through their posts,[10] music listening data that was shared offered a great deal of direction to third-party advertisers looking to reach consumers. On the user end, we simply enjoyed the social practice of sharing music with one another in a public sphere. The irony was that we listened to the music privately in our own homes, but made our choices visible to our friends. The semi-public/private intimacy that social networking sites offered capitalized on the foolishness we sometimes experience as human beings, trapped in a body that sometimes acts in ways counter to good sense.

The larger social networks must have recognized the social value in this practice of music sharing right away. It was not until the introduction of this subscription service that music lovers had an easy way to relate to one another. One concern that tech investor Sean Parker once expressed was that power-users of these social networks, who generated most of the content on the largest site among them, tended to also be "over-sharers," and would end up moving to other websites offering more anonymity and control. He believed that offering these users some way to reach particular groups with shared interests was one way to ensure a social network's survival. Revenue was the incentive, so when he explained what a music sharing network could do for a larger, more general social network, the terms were clear:

> The obvious thing is it gives access to . . . users and it allows music to go massively viral. The social graph has always been a great promulgator of information. We didn't see it as a network of profiles, we always saw it as a way to promulgate media. You saw this with videos . . . But because of licensing issues there was no way to enable that same virality with music.[11]

My sympathies lay with this position, and I was complicit with the sharing that was hoped-for by investors in social networks because my ultimate belief was that social networks and their users shared a symbiotic relationship. I tended to invest too much of myself in these networks, because I felt entitled to developing an online persona and controlling how I was known publicly. I promoted sharing, and I also promoted these networks. But Sean Parker's point gets lost if I let it slip away; the sharing of media took precedence over the profiles themselves, at least from the perspective of the creators of these networks. I suppose users saw it exactly opposite; we shared data about ourselves because we thought our activity said something about our individual personalities. However, from the networks' perspective, we were distributing and advertising products even as we tested and enjoyed them. The data gathering was built into the voluntary whim to socialize with others online, and forgetting that this was the *raison d'être* of the networks ended up creating an ego trap for their users.

I found this out when I stumbled upon the ability to comment on a song that my crush was listening to, which he sent publicly to a social network we shared with all of our friends. I good-naturedly remarked in my comment that I liked the musician, but had not heard this album. He responded immediately, remarking that he liked her too, and we exchanged a few more words about another musician I was listening to. More back and forth comments about music, and if all of our interactions had remained in the sunlight, I would not have ended up in such a mess, but this kind of normalcy is complicated by the online environment. I imagined that my crush liked me, but could not express interest. As a result, the music network became an open window to my imagination. It was similar to the fissured wall for Pyramus and Thisbe, the mythical lovers immortalized in Shakespeare's *A Midsummer Night's Dream.* They could only communicate through a "chink," or a hole in the wall that divided them. Trying to communicate through a social network indirectly, yet publicly, is just like whispering through a crack in a wall. Privately, I began to inhabit this scenario.

After my crush sent me the invitation and I joined as a paying member of the service, I had begun creating a playlist about the sea. Through my private inbox, he sent me "If It's the Beaches" by the Avett Brothers and "The Water is Wide" by James Taylor. Listening to "If It's the Beaches" carried me to a place where I questioned the extent to which songs speak desire. The Avett Brothers croon, "If it's the beaches' sands you want / Then you will have them," and the speaker proceeds to offer the "mountains' bending rivers" and even the "wish to run away." Helping me build a playlist was an innocent way to send the song, though there are a number of other songs he could have chosen to send that were not love songs. Everything I would begin to believe about his use of music to communicate with me was initiated by this choice.

Why not send a note, though? Instead of simply listening to what music someone else likes, why not send him or her a message, an email, or use the phone? Again, my imagination came up with easy answers for this. Direct communication might risk too much, and we might betray something more of ourselves than intended by virtue of our listening habits. I told myself these things, and decided that I would not openly share music with him again on a social network, or "like" any of his songs, even if I did enjoy them. Besides, it was enjoyable to imagine that he preferred secrecy too. It felt like we were pretending to be acquaintances, while something greater formed between us. I was careful to rarely (if ever) post on the social networks we both inhabited, in any way that might be read into, and I made a habit of deleting anything that appeared to pertain to him. I listened to music he liked when I was alone, without sharing my choices openly.

We almost crossed into something more like a real friendship. I became someone he could embrace in greetings and farewells. Once, he expressed concern that questions he asked me about my social network behavior may have seemed "stalkerish." I smiled, realizing that we both had been exploring one another's profiles. Still, each time we achieved a conversational depth, we were interrupted, and we made no plans to be alone. One evening out, he left early, just as it seemed all was going well. zseemed to confirm what I had feared the most. Whatever relationship he wanted with me was too much of a risk for both of us.

Eventually, he stopped coming out with our mutual friends. He always had an excuse to be elsewhere. And gradually, my chances to see him or talk to him alone completely disappeared. The music he listened to gradually began to darken, and at some point, I began to look up the lyrics for songs I did not recognize. They were depressing. Nearly an entire month without seeing someone you are secretly in love with is almost unbearable. The time I spent on social networks increased, and so did my attention to the songs he listened to. The murkiness of lyrical analysis was not lost on me; the changeability of feelings that were sometimes here, sometimes not, on the salty mirage of a wave bank. Other times I was marooned, looking out on a sea of meaning, hoping for any kind of sign that I was not alone.

My every interaction with him in person had been, during that fall, infrequent, but infused with curiosity. He seemed comfortable talking to me, and given my long history of being a loner, I was ill-equipped to understand what this kind of sudden intimacy meant. When he stopped coming out with us, I wondered if he felt pressured to relate with me on a level too intense for mixed company. I wondered if my own secretive tendencies were encouraging him to test the depth of my listening, of my receptivity to him and his worries. An obsession with reading lyrics overtook everything, and I collected as many songs as I could, mining them for symbols that could explain what was happening to our friendship. Naturally, I found proof in everything he listened to, every song he chose to make a favorite, of a relationship he longed for but could not have.

By the time the new year came around, I was wondering if what I was seeing was real. In conversations with a female friend, I worried aloud that I was going crazy, because I felt my crush was trying to communicate with me through music lyrics. She was concerned that I was becoming obsessed and delusional. I continued to draw connections between music and human emotions. My mother always said my father was listening to one album in particular the day he set his glasses down, took up his high-powered rifle and went outside. It was "their" album she said, and I knew some albums to be of the sort that made her cry and drink. I recall other albums that calmed me when I was scared, when my stepfather and mother fought. I usually listened to classical music, Mozart or Bach especially, and wished myself into a home where only classical music, and not Southern rock, was played. I remember when I was a kid there were all these news stories about connections between the music that people listened to and their behavior. Would listening to Judas Priest or Iron Maiden alter my personality? Make it any more likely that I'd kill my parents or worship the devil? After the Columbine Massacre, people would ask the same questions of Marilyn Manson's audience.

I was raised Baptist, and I loved music. When I was bored in church, I'd study the old battered hymnal; I enjoyed many of the songs, and liked speculating about how shape notes were read. In this context, it sometimes seemed as if the music in the Baptist hymnal was the only music the church approved of. I remember drawing a firm line against Baptist views regarding music when I watched a propaganda-laden film accusing Peter Gabriel and Paul Simon of promoting Satanism because they brought African drums into their music regularly. I enjoyed both musicians and felt that my intelligence was being insulted by the film's suggestion, which also displayed a good amount of indirect racism. After that, I attended a meeting once at my schoolmate's church, which was even more fundamentally repressed than my own church had been. There I was told that The Beatles were devil worshippers, and songs from *The White Album* and others by Led Zeppelin were played in reverse to prove this point. Any song sounds demonic when you play it backwards, just like any song's lyrics take on special significance when you are trying to make meaning from them.

Finding meaning where there is none is an aspect of artistic creation that is conceptually valuable. If a writer is trying to compose a story, or a painter is bringing color and form together in a measured way on the canvas, there is an appreciation of arcane symmetry that emerges in the creation of each work. At least, this is what my friend confirmed for me on a day when I had been trying to explain to her the correspondences I saw between the lyrics that my crush was listening to and his state of mind, as I perceived it to be. She reminded me that the writer's mind is always searching for patterns, and it is perfectly natural that I would find significance in particular lyrics, given that my profession calls upon my frequent exercise of this mental faculty. Why would I not begin drawing parallels between me and the listening habits of the man I believed myself to be in love with, especially given good reasons for our remaining inaccessible to one another? Better that it was secret; better that it was forbidden; better, even, that it was frustrated and thwarted desire. I wanted the lyrics to mean something, and as a result, they did.

Throughout that winter, the music he listened to openly—the music that I thought he wanted me to be aware he was listening to (why else make it public?)—seemed despairing, almost suicidal. I told my friend, and she warned me that I might be going too far with my meaning-making. I sincerely hoped that I was, but when someone listens to music over and over again that is draining and semi-confessional of a desire to shoot one's self or drown one's self . . . the fear of being wrong, of reading too much into someone's depression, is eclipsed by the worry of being right. Because of my father's death (accident? suicide?), everyone in my family is sensitive to mood changes in those we care about. It did not feel out of place for me to confide in my friend about my worries. She reassured me that my crush usually listened to dark, morose music, which I found only slightly comforting. The songs continued until one night in particular, when I couldn't suppress my worries any longer. Justin Townes Earle's "Harlem River Blues" appeared as a song he was listening to, and I realized he had listened to it prior to that evening, a day or so before. If this song had appeared as one song among others by the same artist, I might not have noticed. But the song began in an upbeat jaunty rhythm that seemed out of place given the words, "Lord, I'm goin' uptown to the Harlem River to drown." Reading these lines, and imagining that he connected with them was easy, especially since this was not the first or the only song that seemed to convey self-destruction. I realized I was treading on thin ice to invest it with meaning, but I began to do so anyway.

It was 10 p.m. on a Monday night in early January and my son was with his father. I continued to watch what he was listening to, and in my growing unease, I considered the lyrics apart from the music they were embedded into. The clincher was his playing of Damien Rice's "Cold Water," which appeared to ask for help, to a somber background of acoustic guitar and dissonant baritone chorus that in no way could be heard as ironic: "I can't let go of your hand / Lord, can you hear me now? / Or am I lost?" It struck me: I could either sit there and continue researching lyrics and wonder whether any of it meant anything, or I could attempt to interact with him. I knew that he wouldn't notice a song that wasn't among the several he played repeatedly, or wasn't by an artist he recognized. I chose Alexi Murdoch's "Through the Dark," a song that I knew he was familiar with, and played it to see what would happen. The verses, the guitar, the slow and steady rhythm, its sonorous and extended phrasing . . . I meant to convey understanding, across the vast social network of music: "Someone reaching for me now / Through the dark . . ." I thought maybe the lyrics would convey my willingness to comfort him. I ignored the uncertainty provided by some of the lines, especially the final two lines, which were probably more accurate (for being ambiguous) than I realized, claiming to love someone inexpressibly, even though one's heart stands as an obstacle. I may never know if my message was truly received or understood, but immediately after playing this song, at that specific moment, I felt as if he had heard me.

He played a song whose lyrics implore the listener to stay, and not leave. The thought that I had reached out for him and he had responded was reinforced by reading the lyrics to the songs he continued to play that night, as they grew less melancholy. He played Ryan Adams's "Please Do Not Let Me Go," which ends with an entreaty for the hearer to stay, to not leave, and most importantly, to not let go: "True love ain't that hard to find / Not that either one of us will ever know."

After that, he played two songs before quitting for the night, as it was late: Ryan Adams's "Dirty Rain" and Kim Richey's "Careful How You Go." The first was such a tonal change from the other songs, I allowed myself to invest it with meaning, and even now, feel justified in doing so. To move from songs about drowning one's self in a river, to "Last time I was here it was raining / It ain't raining anymore," seemed like movement toward some positive change, a new beginning. The final lines refer to music in a self-conscious way and assertively direct the hearer to something hopeful, as the vocalist moans: "Last time I was here you were crying / You're not crying anymore." The final track he played, Kim Richey's "Careful How You Go," was the last song he listened to openly, and it stayed up all night on the network's feed as the last title he'd listened to, on into the next day: "We don't wanna break the spell just yet / The ice is thin, but maybe it'll hold."

Were these words not enough to believe that something had changed? That we had made contact through music? All of the words together added up to an experience that seemed undeniably meaningful. From self-destruction, to reaching for someone and wanting them to stay, and here at the end, asking the hearer to be careful, to tread quietly, lest the magic be broken . . . My descent into delusion began from the clearest of precepts. Music was a kind of encryption and I had broken the code. Communicating with the man I secretly loved became a game.

If I am a fool for reading lyrics, then I think we have all been foolish. If I believe too much in the possibility for lovers to communicate secretly through songs, I do so only because I wanted to believe it, and felt that I had all of the proof I needed. Unfortunately, dreams fade and do not linger, and morning's light does much to erase the beauty of the night before. Even though I had what I felt was proof, when I tried to explain what had happened that night to my aunt, or my mother, or my friend, each of them expressed concern. Knowing what I know now, it might have been better had I dismissed everything without trying. From that night on, the songs he played were happier, and did not cross into depression, though there were songs of disappointment, worry, and in particular, impatience. One song that he played over and over again, "Wait" by Alexi Murdoch, lyrically implores, nearly thirty times in the same song, for the listener to wait, "If I can't be, all that I could be."

The night after I felt that I had made contact with him, I had what can only be described as a musical erotic experience. He began the night listening to Whiskeytown's rollicking and honkytonk-reminiscent "Excuse Me While I Break My Own Heart," with slide-guitar accompanied lines suggesting that "the situation," which doesn't seem right, "keeps me drinking every goddamn day and night." The next song he listened to, one that I had played many times before and considered a favorite, appeared to explicitly speak to a closeted desire for sexual contact. Damien Rice's immaculately forlorn "Delicate" chronicles the clandestine desires of a speaker to a paramour. "We might kiss when we are alone / When nobody's watching" speaks directly to the furtive desires that two lovers might feel when they cannot see each other openly. As the lyrics continue, the story unfolds: "It's not that we're scared / It's just that it's delicate," explaining that it is not fear that prevents them from being together, but rather the precariousness of the situation. I ponder these lyrics now, knowing more than I did then. This disappointed lover became me, in my overidentification; one who had counted on lyrics to say what should ideally come from someone directly. The song continues to explore whether one's sadness can be filled by borrowed words, and always the question of whether one can truly say "hallelujah" if it's meaningless, and . . . why sing at all?

When I first saw this song appear among those that he was listening to, I was convinced that he had seen me play it once before (because I had, repeatedly), and that he wanted me to know he was there, speaking these words directly to me. Who *else* would he address? And why, with this beautiful, fragile, and haunting song? Whenever I see the word "hallelujah" in lyrics, I think of Leonard Cohen's song by the same name, and Jeff Buckley's exquisite cover of it. When I hear *hallelujah,* I know what it means to have earth and heaven exist in the same space, in real time, if even for a moment, and the pain of having that moment be the passing, fleeting glimpse of what faith must sustain forever past it. But I only know this because of this song, and the ways the music itself provides a setting of divine ecstasy despite the carnality of physical love, rendered holy, if at least for the duration of its performance. (The guitar and the pained sighs of Jeff Buckley tell me so.) The ethereal presences of Buckley's voice and Cohen's words intertwine, so that I see the lyrics, both performances, and the melodic experience as singular: "Love is not a victory march / it's a cold and broken hallelujah."

The lines from Cohen that come closest to the use of "hallelujah" in the song above—the ones that feel most like an allusion—are intoxicated with Eros: "Remember when I moved in you / And the holy dove was moving too? / And every breath we drew was hallelujah?" I'm not sure that any dedicated music lover can hear the word "hallelujah" and not think of these lines by Leonard Cohen, or perhaps also, Jeff Buckley's interpretation of them. Furthermore, how could any song like Damian Rice's "Delicate," with this level of allusion operating so casually through lyrics as deeply intimate as they are beautiful, ever be seen as a neutral musical choice to play in public on social media?

During the time I was formulating my views concerning communication through song lyrics, I was speculating that music was rarely, if ever, played for entirely neutral reasons. If I throw a dance party, I am going to choose songs that encourage listeners to move. If I am unhappy, I may choose to listen to music that will either match my mood, or cheer me up. If I am in love, I will most certainly play songs that speak to that murky feeling that I carry inside, whether I feel celebratory, estranged, rejected, or lonely. When had I ever listened to music without some kind of preference, or some kind of desire, for it to mean something to me and to either reinforce or challenge my inner state? If the man I believed myself to be in love with was truly listening to music without intention, why would his choices not be more variable?

Over time, I realized that the closest any listener could come to neutrality was the practice of listening without intention regarding song order, such as that involving chronological listening: a discography or a whole album. Though particular albums are capable of expressing any range of semiotic qualities, listening to an album out of order, or pulling only certain songs from an album more obviously approaches an expression of intention. Even a hint of intention renders our listening habits non-neutral to observers, provided they look closely enough.

By making one's listening publicly visible, one invites an assumption of intention to communicate a song's semiotic value to others. The most basic expression of this semiotic value is communal: "I want to share this experience with you." Whether the singular or universal "you" is inferred is another matter. The universal "you" is understood when there is no context for reading any other specific social relationship.

I may be assuming a shared understanding in all of this talk of "neutrality" or "intention" and "semiotic value." To say that something has a *semiotic value* is to say that it is a sign for something else, in the same way a word is a sign for a meaning that is understood by speakers of that word's language. Aesthetic value, which I think contains the value I refer to as semiotic, is rooted in expression of personal experience. Though my view may be a moldy, outdated one, I side with American humanist, educator, and philosopher John Dewey on this matter, who apparently found a kindred soul in Russian novelist Leo Tolstoy:

> Those who are moved feel, as Tolstoi says, that what the work expresses is as if it were something one had oneself been longing to express. Meantime, the artist works to create an audience to which he does communicate. In the end, works of art are the only media of complete and unhindered communication between man and man that can occur in a world full of gulfs and walls that limit experience.[12]

Original, compelling works of art that move me, whether they be literary, symbolic, auditory, or visual in nature, approach something of what Dewey references here from Tolstoy. They express something that I myself have longed to express, in a way that makes me wish to appropriate their aesthetic value. If this sounds selfish or philistine, consider what social media came to mean for those who loved art. The experience of hearing a musician play live music was replaced by the immediately available video or downloadable mp3; the experience of seeing a work of art in person was made easier by searching for it online and posting the image to social media. I could enjoy a favorite album and share that enjoyment publicly, having never purchased a physical copy of the recording. Other social networks built around the accumulation, collection, and organization of images, took the superficial materialist agenda even further. People tended to convene there to collect ideas about decoration schemes, recipes, or funny memes. Any image could be passed along to one's own boards, reducing images of food or clothing or humor to something like trading cards that were endlessly replicated and exchangeable. Saving the image was like having the desired object or experience itself. Endless other networks catered to people's interests in knowing, sharing, and saving images and ideas.

Walter Benjamin's landmark essay "Art in the Age of Mechanical Reproduction" in a more critical way addresses what the effect of the collector's impulse might become in the age of social media. By digitally extracting a work of art from its original context, a live performance, let's say, we imbue it with a new meaning that has more to do with its availability and the use we can make of it (such as selling something or communicating a meaning), that makes better sense in the new context of our use. When he writes that "the camera introduces us to unconscious optics as does psychoanalysis to unconscious impulses," I substitute *song* for camera and *feelings* for optics. The result is as close to an articulation of the strange ability for songs to convey unconscious messages as much as they do the ones we hear. In the digital age we no longer thought about the artist, or what a song might have meant to the one who wrote it. Certainly we did not consider for long whether the artist was being paid for the songs we streamed; only that they were available for us to consume and reorder and share for our own purposes, however petty or vain.

I wonder now whether the music sharing networks changed the music that was being produced at that time, by creating a new aesthetic that was subject to consumers' tastes on a large scale. This question extends far beyond what I'm trying to figure out about my use of the service, but it remains a valuable consideration for someone to take up. The possibility is supported by the near surety that most users of social networks cared less about the economic, sociological, and psychological arrangements they entered into (however indirectly) with *millions* of other human beings than their own private utilitarian interests. This was how we were able to behave in an almost natural fashion with our "friends" or "followers." On social networks, we assumed that all of our friends were monitoring our activities, and if one friend commented on my post, then all of her friends could see not only her comment, but my post as well, and so on, and so on. If I played a song openly, I knew that every network friend who shared that service could potentially see that song, and additionally, any other user who had added me as a favorite could see as well. So why did any of this matter? What could a song express about someone's feelings? What could a series of songs mean? Was it possible that we could reveal much more about our personal lives through social music sharing than any of the other networks we belonged to? I certainly thought so at the time.

As a paying subscriber I was able to interact socially via music, and this included occasionally using music to express something about how I was *feeling*. As a writer, I do not struggle to express myself through words. But music is something greater to me, and has always been my means for healing myself, for protecting myself, and even, sometimes, for punishing myself. Music is often intensely private for some people. We may be afraid that people will judge us based on what we listen to. Or maybe we feel that people will read too much into our musical choices. Sometimes we *want* people to read into them. Remember the last time someone said, "You HAVE to hear this song. Just listen." And whatever you were doing, you stopped, because you understood how meaningful this song had become for this person. It's like when someone tells you about a dream from the night before; the important thing may not be the content, but your listening, and what it means for you to listen on the behalf of the person who asked to share this dream with you. Recall too, the first time you stayed up all night putting together a mixtape, CD, or playlist for someone else. What could motivate any of us to share the music we listen to and enjoy? None of us are so pure that we share information about ourselves without wanting something in return.

Like Cyrano de Bergerac, we all have features that we hope to hide in our searches for love and understanding. Maybe we are unattractive, shy, or we have no words for what we want to say. We cannot stand on a stage and announce to all of the world our love for this or that person, though we wish we could, were we brave enough. Like the paramour in the play *about* Cyrano de Bergerac, we sometimes lack the artistry to tell our loves exactly what we feel for them, in the way that they will best understand. We cannot write a letter, we cannot say what we dearly hope to express. We ask someone else to do it for us, and in the end, betray ourselves when the beloved recipient loves the message more than us, or cannot know who the message is really from. That is how music, lyric, and poetry come to be employed in the service of love—to express indirectly (and sometimes secretly) what we cannot express directly, or in the transparency of our lives as they are lived.

When I reread sections of John Dewey's *Art as Experience,* I am reminded that Dewey is said to have been tone deaf, which means he could not hear musical tones. But when he writes about art, I include music among his inferred mediums almost unconsciously, in the same way that I think about writing when Igor Stravinsky discusses musical composition in the lectures which form his *Poetics of Music.* There is a trace of synesthesia in the global apprehension of any aesthetic theory. What we say *about* art—how it is made, how it is received, what it means—can be assured of its translatability to anything else we consider art. Even though Dewey must have been referring to visual art in his examples, he says in many ways what I have said elsewhere in this essay: "The work of art certainly does not have that [meaning] which is had by flags when used to signal another ship. But it does have that possessed by flags when they are used to decorate the deck of a ship for a dance."[13]

Tonally, the meaning of art is conveyed in ways appropriate to the medium. Visual art conveys its meaning through form, line, and color. These speak to whomever listens and knows the signs. The qualities inherent in each kind of work help the critic to explain it, and help the audience appreciate it. In no way does a work of art, or a song (to be specific), convey a stable meaning. Even the most concrete of lyrics can be subverted by a melody or delivery that betrays an ironic hearing of them. Still—we know almost immediately whether the song we listen to is happy or sad, and if it be either, we assume that a choice to listen conveys some kind of intention to share in or consider that experience. All this to say, based on my observations of music sharing networks, I came to believe that I knew why the man I thought I loved listened to the music he did, and I felt myself to be his intended audience for this information. Lines in lyrics I referenced continued to point to the specific discovery I had made: that music played openly on social networks could be read to mean something more, at least between people who knew each other more closely on these same interconnected networks.

Where was I? Ah yes . . . *Eros.* There was the problem of a mutual friend who seemed to know about my attraction for this man, and this listener was also on the same network. Add to that the peril created by this person's newly formed friendship with me, and listening to music at the same time that my crush and I listened to music. What to do? I figured that the lag in the network's feed was great enough to try something different, that might convey my "messages" more quickly, without my listening to songs openly for everyone to see. I added songs to a visible list at the top of my profile. I imagined that the man I followed was aware that I was adding songs to the list, since I imagined that he was refreshing my profile page as often as I was his. In the meantime, I listened to songs he played, and then added them, to show that I was aware of and liked the same songs he did. It seemed as though he understood, because the songs began to advance in emotional intensity. The proof I needed was in his playing of "Fall at Your Feet," a cover by Boy and Bear of a Crowded House song, which I quickly added to my list, entirely visible to anyone checking my page: "I'm really close tonight," says the speaker in the song, "And I feel like I'm moving inside her."

The song begins with an insistent banjo, and then progresses climatically. Beyond that, there's an expression of desire that intends to support the beloved with help, with much-needed aid. The speaker promises to be there when she needs him, and he will fall at her feet: "Words don't sound right / But I hear them all moving inside you." Because words were all I had, and because songs were the only way I had found to express them, I began to cry when I heard this song, and played it secretly to myself a second time. The unfairness of this forced secrecy, my own inadequacies to love anyone without complexity; all were visited on me at that moment. Still the lyrics continued, announcing that blame had turned inward, and the speaker of the song was sacrificing himself, asking if his presence or help were even needed. The speaker in the song rapidly became the man I desired, as did all the voices of all the songs he played.

Of course, I believed I loved him absolutely by this point. Every failed relationship coalesced into this one possibility: that I had found someone who understood me completely, who had so quickly figured out a way to communicate with me that I could immediately understand and relate to. Unafraid, I added a song to the top of my list that I thought expressed my own willingness to play the game: "Night Time" by The xx. Sophisticated, erotic, it begins slowly, then escalates: "Can I confess these things to you . . ." The vocalist is breathy, as the tempo increases . . ." So I'll tell the truth / I'll give it up to you . . ."

After each repetition of the chorus the beat speeds up and advances the aim of the song: to communicate a desire for physical love in an obvious way, represented lyrically, melodically, rhythmically. After I added this song to my playlist, I noticed that he ceased playing music for several minutes. At that moment, I admit my own incapacity to continue. His disappearance was not only expected, but a confirmation that what we had both experienced was a physical, real relation, a simultaneously erotic relation via music. When he returned to playing songs openly, it was Matthew Perryman Jones's "Until the Last Falling Star," which I quickly added to my playlist, and promptly moved to the top as I'd been doing all evening. Apparently, reality had set in, and I was reminded that whatever I had hoped for was impossible, given our circumstances. The speaker in this song forlornly admits that "If there was a chance / That we could be lovers," he would write a book of letters to his beloved and set them all on fire, "Just to start over again."

By this point, there was no question (in my mind) that our relation was genuine. I had begun keeping a notebook, and recorded the titles of each song faithfully, sometimes copy-pasting the lyrics into a folder of text files. I kept the notebook because I wanted to be sure that my imagination wasn't leading me into delusion; I thought that having a continuous record of my observations was evidence. (In this way I was like any other paranoid, obsessive person who faces the doubt of others.) Though I recognized even then that reading into music is itself an illusory system, I maintained faith in my ability to self-analyze, and catch my neuroses at play. I had begun smoking cigarettes again three months before, on the night he had first told me about the music network. Though I knew that smoking was a warning sign that things weren't quite right with me, I continued to assert that what I observed lyrically was unassailably obvious. My closest friend and I continued to have conversations about my developing obsession, and she remained unsure whether it was healthy. My mother didn't understand, and neither did my aunts.

My friend's reasoning made the most sense. She pointed out that as writers, we were professionals at reading into prose, verse, or lyric, and as writers, equally adept at building meaning and narrative. Her concern was that my skills for meaning-making were out of balance, approaching what can only be described as "ideas of reference": a belief that everything I perceived, ultimately meant something to me personally, or referred to me directly. It's what we mean when we say that someone is reading too much into something, or when we admonish someone with the words, "it isn't always about you." Except, true ideas of reference typically involve things that are not causally related to our lives at all, or are apparently random, like those days when I felt that the weather was meaningfully reactive with my mood, or when the song playing in the grocery store was the same song I was listening to in the car. Whenever I feel those experiences to be meaningful I typically recognize them as neurotic. But I also embrace a belief in meaningful coincidences and synchronicity. Is this an admission of instability?

Though respected philosophical traditions acknowledge interconnectedness in the universe, much of mainstream psychology rejects it. This is what I probably thought, but didn't say in defense of my thinking. When a belief or activity becomes self-destructive for me, that's when I begin to draw lines. Was I there yet? Was I ready to see the smoking and the drinking (forgot to mention that!) and the lyric-reading and the note-taking as legitimate expressions of a neurotic complex pushed beyond what was healthy or normal for me? The only thing preventing my potential ideas of reference from becoming delusions was my ability to find alternative explanations for beliefs I began to hold: that this man was communicating with me through music (that he listened to on our shared network), and that he was expressing interest in me as a romantic partner. I was beginning to fail with regard to finding alternate explanations tenable; it made far more sense that we were using music to communicate secretly and that there was a mutual, though suppressed attraction between us. The secrecy should have tipped me off that something was terribly wrong.

In full-blown psychosis, ideas of reference can lead to delusions of reference when reality is not being used to effectively test ideas. If he liked me, why did he not tell me so directly, instead of telling my friend, thereby involving a third person? If he wanted me to "read into" a particular song, why not send them to me privately, since the network allowed their users this kind of direct messaging? He had done so before: why not again? I had an elaborate reasoning that seemed to answer all of these questions, which I find a bit disturbing now. In fact, because delusions of reference are symptomatic of a host of illnesses including schizophrenia and bipolar disorder, in hindsight I look to these considerations and must take them seriously if I'm going to be honest with myself. The mania associated with bipolar disorder accurately described how I felt most days during that time, and I had also begun to take diet pills again (which sped me up, counteracted my depression, and made me slightly manic)—all of this adds up to the perfect conditions for developing ideas of reference into delusions. Because ideas of reference are linked to the superego, the meaning-making, sign-reading area of my consciousness was affected. Of course I might see a language that did not exist. Of course I might also imagine that I could understand it.

More likely, other theories point to my drawing deep, psychological associations between the man I thought I loved and my dead father. I have always tended to fall in love with people who are remote from me, or unavailable, out of fear that anyone I love might leave me. What if my adoration of this unavailable man was yet another one of those instances? What if my liking him threw me into anxiety, because I knew what was to come? Perhaps I was exhibiting defense mechanisms that could be classified as "immature": fantasy, idealization, projective identification. I had done this before. Or perhaps I was merely exhibiting "neurotic" mechanisms: intellectualization (writing an essay for instance); dissociation (retreating to my social network alias for a period of time, as I did for an entire month). No—at my best, I was advancing to a mature understanding of my situation. But there was still so much I had to go through, and at that moment I was convinced that whether or not it was real, there was certainly enough evidence to suggest that communication via music was possible.

: :

Though I had my reasons for believing in what I observed, conversations with my confidant began to push me back into wondering. Was I going out of my head? Was I projecting onto this man the feelings I wished he had for me? Maybe. But back to the song, "Until the Last Falling Star." How could this not be intentional? Why would someone listen to this song if he didn't feel it? "Oh love / Where have you been? / I'll wait for your lead to come in." Who was the "love" he thought of when he listened to this song?

As for the songs we had listened to together, in the sequence they appeared; given that he was listening to these songs openly, so that I could see them, why should they not be for me? When lyrics ask, "where have you been?," what is the lover's answer? When lyrics show a speaker wanting to believe that there is a way into the listener's heart, who doesn't hear the words and interpret them as meant for her?

I struggled to understand how ambiguity of feeling was even possible at that point. As far as I was concerned we had expressed our desires, and we knew what we wanted with each other. How was it possible that we had to continue with the secrecy? Plenty of people have learned how to justify adulterous or unhealthy relationships. Although he and I were in fairly arbitrary (and not entirely unethical) positions with regard to the forbidden nature of our relations, perhaps I had been underestimating the barrier between us. I speculated that each of us had so much to lose, there was no potential for trespassing boundaries, though we could continue playing music expressing our futility as a way of relieving the pain of separation. My belief in this relation felt real to me in that moment, though as time passes, and I write these words, the feeling grows fainter. What I mistook for his persistent desire to stay secretive was something else entirely, though I did not know it yet.

By this point, I was entirely obsessed with our music network. I saw it as the only link between my solitary life and the one man I could imagine being right for me. I developed the idea for a book about music, and began to announce my project on social media as a way of explaining my new addiction to music in academic terms. I claimed that whatever preoccupation I had for music sharing, existed only in this newfound means for writing about music in the context of Bach and his fugues. All of my peers knew about my project, which I hoped would cover for my obsessive attention to the music network and the inordinate amount of listening I was doing as a result. What I didn't account for was the possibility that other factors, such as my lack of sleep, was evidence that I was falling apart.

Three days after our (assumed) erotic musical interchange, he began to repetitively listen to a list of songs that he had bookmarked as favorites. It took me a while to realize that there was no intentionality behind his choice of songs. This continued for several days, and even though certain songs seemed to speak to me, I wondered what had changed, and if nothing had changed, I wondered where the intention had gone, and why the repetitive listening to this particular list had overtaken everything else.

Still, I was able to find meaning in the songs that he chose to listen to over and over, every day. Every song was about love. One song admitted that winning wasn't what was important any more. Another proclaimed "I'm still in love with you . . . I'm going crazy." Still another repeated in a wafting acoustic, that the speaker was born to hold the listener in his arms. Days later, he listened to one song, and left its title up for two days without playing anything else openly. This song, which repeats the lines, "In your love, my salvation lies" also admits to being tired and brokenhearted. Then, those lines that I felt most relevant and communicative, discussed a speaker missing the listener when he is alone. Almost a week later, there was the addition of another song to his list, about being "married" by the ocean, and remaining strong for one another. When I recalled the song he had sent me several months before, when I had first begun using the service, and when I studied the lyrics of the song he was playing at that moment, the confusion was temporarily gone, and replaced with the calm security that the lyrics to "Tethered" by Sleeping at Last brought me: "I'll be calm when you have had enough of these rushing waves / You'll be the oxygen I need." I continued to read into every interaction, and whenever I doubted how I *thought* he felt, I had only to listen to the opening verses of "If It's the Beaches," the song he had sent me privately months before: "I swear that I will do my best to be here / just the way you like it." And that was enough to go on for a long time, at least for me.

: :

During the same period I recorded these songs in my notes, I ended up connected to a woman, a mutual acquaintance of the man I was in love with, whom I did not know well at all. According to what I could find out about her on our shared social network, she was in a situation similar to my own (neither of us could have a relationship with this man that existed fully in the open) though in her case, the stakes were much higher, and the forbidden nature of their relationship crossed into ethical grounds. Whatever feelings she had for him or he for her would require an alternative means of expression, which was the condition I had found in music sharing. I would never have noticed her had I not begun to observe her listening to music at the same time as the man I thought I loved, every morning. This habit of hers had not been visible to me before our network "friendship." My interest was piqued, and I looked more closely at her song lists. In more than one instance, she had enjoyed songs that my crush also liked, and the overlap was so great, my heart plummeted. The song "Delicate," which I had invested with meaning as evidence of a secret desire was among her highlighted list, from months before. The fact that she had listened to so many songs after he had listened to them first, and vice versa, revealed something . . . but I didn't know what, exactly. When I asked around among the people I knew, it was confirmed that the two of them had been friends for years. There was no accident behind their shared musical interests, and no attempts to be secretive. They were often seen together, laughing and joking, even going out for live music events, though it put them in danger of discovery.

And of my crush? What did I think of him? The night we had gone out with mutual friends the first time, I remembered the group's semi-comic discussion about a man's fantasy of being in bed with two women simultaneously. Met with great hilarity, he mentioned that he was a "man with a plan," inferring that he had a plan for getting two women in his bed at once—an idea that had seemed funny at the moment, but was rapidly losing its humor the more I thought about how things had played out on our social network. Was it possible for two—no—*three people* to have a relationship solely through music on a social network? How many other people have, via social networks, imagined exclusive relationships that later turned out to be alternate forms of friendship, or emotional affairs bordering on adultery? It's not that unusual for people to murder one another over events that take place primarily on a social network. But we say about these people that they are mentally ill, or that they must have no lives if they spend that much time online. But here I was, fully invested in an imaginary relationship that had existed only in brief encounters offline, and obsessive lyrical analysis when online. One step further: I felt the sting of rejection, of being someone's Echo, of seeing someone else who was also an Echo, and a solitary Narcissus at the center of it, too preoccupied with the self-expression music provided him with to notice the perilous situation of being caught between two women.

As everything became clearer, I became jealous and angry. What I had believed to be intended for me had been for someone else. Nearly every band or artist that I liked, she also liked, either on her social network profile page, or within her main songlists. Her list of songs she played frequently was almost a mirror duplicate of his. She would listen to a song and highlight it. Two days later, he would listen to the same song and highlight it. Or the reverse. They indirectly collaborated to build playlists of songs about loneliness and love and desire. Every song he had played (that I had analyzed) appeared in her lists too. Whatever I had read in his behavior as significant was also true of her. I suddenly felt as if I could not listen to any of the artists or songs on their playlists, since doing so would make me think of her.

One morning, I saw the two of them listening to music openly, at the same time. It usually began the same way—he would begin listening first, and he would listen to two or three songs openly before she would appear too, playing songs that were either on his highlighted song list, or her own. When I looked on the music service at his listening habits (data sent by the network and managed by each user), I saw that he had listened to one of her song lists "69 times." I began to record their interactions in a systematic way. My justification for doing so was based on their voluntary publicity. If keeping their activities secret had ever been a priority, why were they broadcasting every song they played publicly? Why was he unconcerned about the social networks' music sharing data showing the attention he paid to her playlists? What was going on? How long had they been sharing music this intimately? Or did they just happen to like the same songs about forlorn love and loneliness? I asked these questions over and over, developing ire for both of them, as I had blundered unwittingly into their drama, and felt somewhat led there. *Had he been playing a game with both of us?* The more I considered this motive, the angrier and more vindictive I became.

I played music openly, so they could see my choices, during times when they both were also present on the music service. Once, he had begun listening to a new album, which she began to listen to, and unable to resist, I began listening to the same album too, publicly. Any outside observer who didn't know the connections we all shared, would have seen three people listening to the same songs, on the same album, at the same time. I saw this as a game played on a social network involving two women, both apparently too oblivious to grasp the ways they were interchangeable, or perhaps more likely, in my case if not hers—irrelevant. Surely my presence had never been meaningful to him before. This was a difficult idea to accept. And soon, because she could see my listening habits as well, she figured out the attraction I held for him, and without knowing for sure, perhaps assumed there to be mutuality of affection. Regardless, we had some harrowing moments on the network, enacting the musical equivalent of a cat fight *through music* on a Sunday morning that I would not have believed possible prior to my observations and note-taking.

It began innocently enough; I was playing an upbeat song one morning, at a time when both of them were listening to an album together. Nothing was out of sorts until she played "Start a War" by The National. The title alone made me pay attention. Soon, I was looking up lyrics and noticing a threatening pattern. In "Gila" by Beach House, the lyrics warn, "Pick apart the past, you're not going back." Feeling attacked, my morning deviated into lyrical analysis once again, but this time the songs were not about love.

After "This Is Why We Fight" by The Decemberists ("Come the war / Come hell / Come attrition / Come the reek of bones"), my own music listening escalated into anger and insult. Of Montreal's "Coquet Coquette" was my way of calling her a flirt and a whore. Okkervil River's "Piratess" expressed my belief that she was a hijacker, a thief. "Waiting Room" by Fugazi, "DNA" by The Kills, "At Home He's a Tourist" by Gang of Four, "Ted Just Admit It" and "Sympathy" by Jane's Addiction communicated my rage in a way that would have stood out to anyone that Sunday morning as atypical listening for me. By the time I was playing "Freedom" by Rage

Against the Machine and "Ho Chi Minh" by Last Poets, I was beyond consolation. She had played a series of songs that had led me to each of my own musical choices, with lyrics that were frequently threatening. In "Set Your Arms Down" by Warpaint, the scene is a back porch with "a pocket of pocket knives," and the imperative that the listener fight: "There is no hiding / To save your life."

Then there was "Silver Trembling Hands" by The Flaming Lips: ("Dagger / Night fight / Tomorrow / She forgets about the fear") or even in "California Girls" by The Magnetic Fields, I heard hatred and anger toward other women: "I have planned my grand attacks / I will stand behind their backs with my brand-new battle ax / Then they will they taste my wrath." All the while, he merely watched, listening to the same bland list of starred songs that had become standard fare for him while she played "Daughters of the Soho Riots" by The National: "You must have known I'd do this someday / Break my arms around the one I love / And be forgiven by the time my lover comes."

Surely by this point I was fuming along with Rage Against the Machine, even as I looked up her lyrics and felt personally attacked by them. After I heard the first person pronominal threats in "Untitled" by Interpol, paranoia set in. What if she was capable of hurting me?: "Oh, I will surprise you sometime / I'll come around when you're down."

I messaged my closest female friend and told her everything that was happening. I also captured the lyrics with screen shots, so that if there were ever an interaction between the two of us outside of a social network, there would be some kind of evidence of a threatening encounter. Finally, my confidant believed me about communication through music, especially when she read the same lyrics I was seeing on my screen repeatedly, as I looked them up. Everything had gone too far, and my friend urged me to avoid interacting with this woman online. As soon as we both stopped playing music, I calmed down. I spent days thinking about how quickly jealousy had taken my humanity and my reason from me, had made me willing to bare my teeth over a man who had never expressed direct interest in me. It was too much, too out of proportion. I had reached the ultimate end of my delusion, and as the weeks stretched on, I began to more passively watch their interactions without interfering.

They had a rhythm of advance and retreat. Sometimes it seemed as if she led him on, but fled when he got too close. Sometimes he seemed to pout, if she didn't play music with him or wasn't listening to music openly. Sometimes the songs they played back and forth seemed to communicate disappointment or the end of a thwarted love affair, of something that had almost come to fruition, but then had failed to coalesce. She played songs like Bright Eyes's "Lover I Don't Have to Love" ("Do you like to hurt? / I do, I do / Then hurt me") or "My Losing Bet" by The Avett Brothers ("After all the love how did I end up here?").

The most intriguing of all the changes came about when I decided I was tired of following their every move. I had unfriended both of them on social networks for a time, but then could still see what they listened to. I felt trapped. I couldn't delete either of them from my favorites. Eventually I connected with him again, and then much later, her too. I tried to make it appear casual, as if I had "accidentally" dropped contact. It didn't matter; the futility and the insult of the whole affair was beginning to wear on me. I began to listen to particular albums obsessively, then deactivated from social networks entirely. As a result, my music service account was deactivated as well. I moved over to an alias account and played music privately. I was gone for almost an entire month.

If I had managed to stay gone completely, I might not have noticed that the man I had imagined myself in love with stopped listening to music openly on the service the day I left. I logged back onto social networks from time to time and noticed these small things. That I could reactivate and find that I'd missed nothing, other than her posts, and the increasingly sad and dejected songs she played for everyone to see. Still, nothing from him. Was there any reason for this change? Was my departure from social media in any way a discouragement? As I looked back over all of my notes and collected lyrics, I felt like the fool I had certainly become as a result of my projections. I pondered the ethics of writing about their longing that could only be expressed through music, even as I understood the fact that everything they had done was in a public environment, visible to anyone who knew them both as mutual friends.

Still, I seriously considered a new fortune cookie that I promptly taped over my sink: "Wisdom is knowing what to do with what you know." For me, as a nonfiction writer, that advice meant everything. Still, I'm not sure if the story I'm telling here is about me, about them, or about the hazards of social networks.

Near the end of the month I spent apart from social media, I attended a party and the man I had once thought I loved was there, and nervously hugged me when he arrived late. After nearly an hour of skirting one another, and socializing around the possibility of sitting together, we went with the naturalness of friendship and shared a table. Days later, I returned to social networking, and he and I were out again with mutual friends, as we had been months before, finally seeming to relax a bit in one another's company.

By then, friends were beginning to comment on what they saw as mutual attraction between the two of us. But I could not be sure. I began to fear that he was using his association with me for other purposes. Maybe I was suddenly a part of a love triangle between him and the other woman. I had assumed that he knew how long I had liked him. I had also assumed that he knew I was aware of his involvement with her on the music service.

When I saw how messed up it was all becoming, I decided to tell him everything about what I knew and how I felt. I will not relate the details of our conversation, nor will I comment on how my sympathies were stirred, or for whom. I had been right about everything except his feelings for me. After talking that night, we corresponded privately for two weeks or so, and then just as suddenly, stopped. What I had felt for him did not leave immediately. All of his activity on the music service ceased for the most part, and he hid his song lists from the network for a long, long time. No longer did he listen to the same music with anyone, openly. The other woman continued long after to listen to sad or angry songs of love's betrayal. Eventually I stopped looking up the lyrics to the songs she played, and felt sorry for her. Sometimes I wondered if I'd done the right thing by speaking to him directly, but for the two weeks we wrote to one another, I was happier and more relieved than I'd been for years.

Now, I recall the excitement with which I had encountered the freedom of the music network at first, and how easy it was to imagine that the one person I had come to care for shared the same feelings, and that he was willing to use music to communicate them. I think back to all of the times in my life when music told the story of a relationship—between me and my dead father, or between me and my mother. The song the preacher sang at my grandmother's funeral: the one she had always loved hearing him sing, gently accompanied by his acoustic guitar. The music that I listened to when I was eighteen that I cannot hear now without being overwhelmed with melancholy. Other songs that remind me of people I had once been in love with that put me in tears. The mix CDs that a lover secretly gave me when I was leaving my husband . . . the mixtapes my friends and I made for each other in the 90s. What can I say?

Music is rarely neutral, but typically ambiguous in the way it touches us; one person's lyric may simply be someone else's background color. Or, the love song you believe was played for you may be intended for someone else. At the least, I question whether social networks brought people together, or drove them further apart. The limits of human psychology are such that I believe us better creatures offline, listening to music by campfires or in concert halls, or together with our lovers in bed, cradled skin to skin. We need the presence of others to help us make sense of what we hear, insofar that music is social. Else, let us be alone, dancing like witches with the shades drawn.

SPECTATOR AT A
TRAIN WRECK

One night, I dreamt that my nine-year-old son and I were on a slow-moving train that made frequent stops in tourist towns. We had stepped from the train, and holding hands, made our way across the train yard, a matrix of tracks. Hands locked, I was afraid of losing him, of his slipping into the path of something I couldn't stop.

A train that seemed to be ours began to move slowly out of the yard. I panicked, and in the dream, urged my son and myself into an all-out, frantic run. We leapt onto the accelerating train, only to discover several minutes later that it was not ours, but headed westward, in the opposite direction of where we intended to go.

Dreaming still, I determined that the train was slow enough for us to jump, and we did, walked back to the station, and sat at a shaded table waiting on someone to carry us somewhere familiar and safe. The dream becomes obscured . . . did we board another train? Did we simply stay put, waiting for someone who finally arrived?

The morning after, I tell my mother I dreamed about trains. She remarks with surprise that she did too, that she witnessed a train wreck in her dream. I told her I was working on an essay titled "Spectator at a Train Wreck" and found myself bemused by the synchronicity. What in our shared evening had prompted this string of correspondences?

In my mom's dream, she sees a train begin to wobble, and apparently begin to derail. She remembers asking someone whether they saw it too, as it began to careen. Just then, a horse emerges from no-where, and shoulders her into a wall, saving her life. The train explodes into the air, a metal storm of twisted steel and blistering steam.

I think for a moment about what this means, that we both have dreams about trains, that my son and I escape from a train that has not yet gained its momentum, that we missed our train by catching the wrong one, that we end up safe, only waiting. Dreaming minds passed one another in the night, on separate, similar tracks.

When analyzing dreams, most pop psychologists recognize the need to ask, "What do trains mean to you?" if someone has dreamed about them. We can either accept that a horse is a Freudian symbol of male virility, or ask ourselves what horses are more likely to mean for us each individually. Power? Beauty? Nature? It saved my mother in her dream.

My horse is not your horse, and my trains are not my mom's trains. My train wreck cannot be the same twisted heap as what my mother dreams in her sleeping moments. My train wreck is a series of songs that I've packed meaning into, that have collided in sound. I look up lyrics to songs about trains, my latest obsession.

My train is not her train—the woman who loves the same man I do. My train is not her train. Her train has left, is on its way, in motion. If she were to step from it now, she might survive. She believes love will await her at the station, that she can simply board whatever car she likes without paying.

There is always waiting, sometimes running, just as I ran my few minutes in Leipzig's Bahnhof to the train headed for Dresden, suddenly on different tracks. My Deutsch was limited, but I heard enough to run down those long platforms, to swiftly board the German train, meticulously on time forever. Leipzig, the city where Bach lived from 1723 until his death.

My few minutes in Leipzig do not constitute a stay. My two nights with my grad school lover, directly after my marriage ended, do not constitute an affair. I was running to another train, even then; one that I did jump from two years later, wounding myself (my heart) in the process. These couplings never held, and our separate tracks pull away.

"It's many hundreds of miles and it won't be long" is the refrain the echoing wife repeats, I'm sure, during those moments when she and her Narcissus exchange coldnesses and she mines the heat she feels for another man. Feist and Ben Gifford's "Train Song" speaks the long patience of her desire. I know that desire, was that woman long before.

I sympathize, remembering my summer divorce, a man ten years older than me, the one I thought would make sense of everything I was going through then, who'd bring me home to a new normalcy. What that early self imagines she cannot have. One cannot build happiness on the misery of others—I've tried. There is no making sense of loss.

I listen (listen again) to Levon Helm's "Train Robbery," about Frank and Jesse James. I think of my father, how he would have loved this song. He was not the kind of man to defer in battles of the heart. Neither is my mother one to hesitate in her affections. I am much more in the space of these bitter lyrics: "We will burn your train to cinders / So throw the money on down." So it goes, the pulsing, rhythmic bruise of words that command instead of asking. I'm imagining myself watching, waiting in the cold, "Down in the cut by the old trestle bridge." I am with the horses under the full moon. I long for this clarity, fates decided coolly.

I check my watch. Her train moves north. Fantasy retelling of another's dream: to be a spectator at this train wreck. I am not the woman she thinks I am, and not coming from the station she will never reach, nor am I even on the train that collides with hers. I am free to speculate. I am no one's wife anymore.

Instead I ride many miles east, to a certain ridge I know to overlook a narrow pass. These quiet nights demand attention, and I meditate over the empty canyon. I light my smoke, nudge my horse, and lope into the silent, ever-enveloping dark. I have many more miles to go, but it won't be long, and to hell with riding alone.

METRONOME

Instructions: Please circle T or an F to indicate whether the below aphorisms are (T)rue or (F)alse. If you consider the statement to be a fallacy, draw a line through it.

1. T F When in Rome, there's more than one way to finish a sentence.

2. T F Editors do it in style, prose writers with aplomb, but poets party harder.

3. T F *Ceci n'est pas une pipe,* but sometimes a cigar isn't either.

4. T F A lover is sometimes a beloved.

5. T F Often we quit caring about a game as soon as we know we can't win it.

6. T F Tension is at the root of all pleasure.

7. T F Tension is at the root of all pain.

8. T F Syntax is to prose what sound is to music.

9. T F Both prose and music share *time* as an essential counterpoint.

10. T F My soul is trapped in my throat.

11. T F When I stop to listen to my breath, I hear breathing.

12. T F A little movement is better than none.

13. T F What does not kill us, only gives us something to laugh at later.

14. T F When you see Crazy coming, cross the street.

15. T F All romance is naïve.

16. T F A diver risks more than drowning.

17. T F If a picture is worth a thousand words, aphorisms are worth at least eighty-three.

18. T F If the right eye offends, then you probably broke it.

19. T F A broken heart will often deny turning away first.

20. T F A photo is only a second's grasp on a lifetime of faces.

21. T F Disappointment is a prelude to leaving when the time is right.

22. T F If you can't be a good example at least you can be a dire warning.

23. T F Trauma begins the story but must not end it.

24. T F If you find it once, don't move it after.

25. T F Love bends us toward beauty.

26. T F Ghosts linger by the well of desire.

27. T F When all sound becomes color, the scale becomes spectrums.

28. T F Traces are remnants too small to be measured.

29. T F She had trusted him enough, to be skeptical now, of a heartbreak that happened six months ago.

30. T F She had a dream about a woman who woke up with a new tattoo every morning, until finally she was blue with ink.

31. T F Love has been the punctuation and not the grammar.

32. T F People can have their ashes made into a vinyl album with their favorite songs on them.

33. T F Bartholomäus Traubeck makes discs that play the songs of tree rings.

34. T F Falling in love gets easier as the heart gets softer.

35. T F I find . . . I lost it.

36. T F Self-pity writes one into a tragedy.

37. T F There are many ways of drowning.

38. T F Heartbreak is lonely because it's a kind of grief we experience for someone we used to be, and no one knew that person as well as we did.

39. T F I look at photographs of my former love and I am a ghost in them. I haunt the space of what he does not stand next to.

40. T F Moving on from love is about awakening to greater love and that is why it is terrifying.

41. T F Moving on from loss is about awakening to greater loss and that is why it is terrifying.

Instructions: Please circle the *best* answer from the following dilemmas.

42. An echo is _____. (helpful, annoying)

43. A reflection is _____. (beautiful, precise)

44. I prefer _____. (Bach, Stravinsky)

45. Love is _____. (fleeting, eternal)

46. There are limits to _____. (love, desire)

47. Sweetness _____. (sings, burns)

48. If I were a string I would prefer to be _____. (bowed, plucked)

49. My Love _____. (calls to me, hears me not)

50. The way of longing will make one _____. (colder, burn)

51. The way of life is found through _____. (love, conflict)

52. I prefer a tone to _____. (linger, change)

53. Change makes me feel _____ (alone, angry) most of the time.

54. For the formation of an echo, there must be _____. (distance, a reflective mass)

55. For the formation of an echo, there must be _____. (a reflective mass, intensity of sound)

56. For the formation of an echo, there must be _____. (intensity of sound, quickness)

57. For the formation of an echo, there must be _____. (quickness, distance)

58. An echo originates with _____. (force, precision)

59. An echo begins with _____. (an arrow, the truth)

60. An echo is an arrow that brings _____. (sorrow, sorrow)

61. The lover runs out of _____. (heart, time)

62. Everyone has a _____. (number, word)

63. If I were a time traveler I would visit the _____. (past, future)

64. If I went back in time I would _____ (change, preserve) events.

65. Loneliness is the dark matter of the _____. (soul, body)

66. This present is complicated by _____. (my future, my future)

67. This present is complicated by _____. (my future, my past)

68. This present is complicated by _____. (my future, your future)

69. This present is complicated by _____. (my future, your past)

70. This present is complicated by _____. (my past, my future)

71. This present is complicated by _____. (my past, my past)

72. This present is complicated by _____. (my past, your future)

73. This present is complicated by _____. (my past, your past)

74. This present is complicated by _____. (your future, my future)

75. This present is complicated by _____. (your future, my past)

76. This present is complicated by _____. (your future, your future)

77. This present is complicated by _____. (your future, your past)

78. This present is complicated by _____. (your past, my future)

79. This present is complicated by _____. (your past, my past)

80. This present is complicated by _____. (your past, your future)

81. This present is complicated by _____. (your past, your past)

82. The reader understands _____. (the shifting second person, the abiding first)

83. _____ is the measure of scales and spectrums. (Grammar, Arithmetic)

TENSITY

I. The Tiger Comes Out of the Mountain

When I wrote my master's thesis, I composed every essay in present tense, *in medias res*. My director said this strained my credibility; reflection was impossible in the present. Revision became the hammering out of verbs, the unfolding of tensions created by having been in the moment.

At first, I resisted the changes, as I felt more alive in prose when present. I still compose in the present because it keeps me close to the tools I have for looking back. At some point in my life, editing and reflection became an alchemical process.

When I am in love, I feel myself joined to words as if I am passing into the fire of being. I see a time in the future when all will be ash, and there will be nothing to believe in. But now, just these words exist.

In the future, I will drink greyhounds in a basement with my lover and we will talk about marriages. (We were so young, we imagined conjugal solutions to loneliness.) We will agree to stay content in our separate unpredictable futures, and steer free of confining social narratives.

II. The Great Roc Spreads Its Wings

I write these words now, in the future of my past, the past of my future. My existence is composite material, the cryptological result of processes, pressures, and tensions. Let's map this trigrammatically, I say; let's melt it down, coin the moment, and analyze the tense issues.

My lovers were always one at a time; serial monogamy became my mode. (The string vibrates when plucked, the column of air trembles in the hollows of brass.) All sound was first vibrations, but traveled through space; my heart was once an open column, struck by love.

Now I press the harder questions of my life daily: Will I become a quivering string, will the parametric self sing like an empty bowl? My harmonics are potential partials, provided that love pluck my being, and send my oscillating mind into periodic dances of fundamental frequency.

My lover will embrace me in his kitchen one night in my future, and we will coil like snakes. *No one ever loved me so intensely.* His wife will pass through the hallway to the bathroom, and we will momentarily freeze, our tongues tasting one another's necks.

III. Embracing the Moon

Even though she approves of our passion, we will dash through the pouring rain to the basement. We will smoke a cigarette, listen to music, and argue about polyamory. I will diagram this essay while he demonstrates Bāguàzhǎng, his feet circling, his muscular arms gracefully, artfully martial.

His physical and mental intelligences balance . . . had he ever considered writing a book? He insists that the pleasure is closed to him, because he lives in the moment. Even Socrates argued against writing in the *Phaedrus,* and claimed both memory and dialogue compromised by dependencies on notation.

As for me, I choose writing every day, as part of my being in the world, my awareness. A time may come when my lover is not my lover. Even now, I am in love with two men, perhaps more as each fluctuates between real and ideal.

The ideal will constellate my desire. (I'm broken forever—last night, last week, last year.) I will not know when that time comes, when the ringing stops—or whether the sound a heart makes will bend like a star, whose light is dead, but carries on regardless.

IV. The Green Dragon Stretches Its Claws

I loved a man over a year ago who could not love me back. When I see him now, the tension between us might be something only I feel. He appears permanently on the edge of saying something important to me, but that's most likely my imagination.

He rejected me casually, in a way that was too subtle to make clear sense. I still don't know if he will ever explain what happened. Nevertheless, I will come to see him as someone whom I cannot, and should not pursue, and my lover will agree.

My lover is able to see himself with many women at the same time. I'm sure my ex-husband also imagined himself as someone who could love several women at once. It is the dream of many a man to enjoy multiple women concurrently, or throughout the week.

In the past, I had to choose between lovers, as monogamy required my pronounced fealty. Sometimes it was so clearly between two men—in each case I wondered how it could have proceeded differently. Now, my lover and I talk frequently about a future free of jealousy.

V. The White Monkey Holding the Peach

This idea tempts me, haunts my every thought. What if I agree that my lover can enjoy other women; how will I react when he describes their lovemaking? How will I explain to any other man our arrangement and keep from falling back into old romantic patterns?

One way I dealt with intense jealousy in the past was to imagine the scene, as a spectator. (Will I be able to keep my depression, my lack of confidence, my fears from intruding?) I used to simply shrivel up when I learned of my ex-husband's near-affairs.

My thoughts tumble: I visualize my lover *in flagrante delicto* with someone else, one hand on her hip, another in her hair. (What did I suggest when my husband told me of his infidelity years before? "We will make this an open marriage or we will divorce.")

I still long for the love that will make searching for others redundant. I still believe in being enough woman for one man, my passion sustainable and true. But for the sake of my lover, I will take the fruit he offers and permit him the same.

VI. The Tiger Opens Its Mouth

My lover and I will attempt *compersion,* the emotion that is anti-jealousy, joy we feel when the ones we love are happy. (I recall my mother's tale of grinding a woman's face into her mobile home's gravel driveway. My grandmother did the same to a rival once.)

As for my own marital jealousy, I passed my husband's fling in the hallway at school once, and saw her poison ivy–speckled face as proof. Amused, I smiled at her. I will most likely never meet the women my lover chooses. This thought neither comforts nor disturbs.

I think of Michelle Yeoh in *The Tai Chi Master,* playing forlornly on a *sanxion,* a three-stringed Chinese banjo. In the film, her husband's new wife will fight Yeoh until the husband crowns Yeoh with a barstool. He had given her the sanxion, and refused its return.

I will always see Yeoh in this film as a tragic hero, as in *Crouching Tiger, Hidden Dragon.* My lover will try to convince me that Yeoh's true love in the film desires the young antagonist. But I remember his devotion to Yeoh: enduring till the end.

VII. The Bear Stretches Its Claws

The strings were plucked, my heart vibrated for months. I will not follow the sound until it lands before my lover's circling feet, that trace the *bagua*. I will not consult the *I Ching* for our future, but will instead study his movements, physical meditations in silence.

I will secretly walk my own circle, careful to step straight with my right foot, and bring the left across. I will seek balance in my lover's vision for our future. He says to me late one night, "we grow by tensions created by the *chi* body."

I will try to believe him, put faith in his gentleness, his love that seems boundless. (I had forgotten the discipline of relinquishing possession of what one loves.) I recognize he is not mine, nor I his, just as we cannot own light or music or happiness.

But I cried one night in his bed, when my tenuous dream of having found a home in him disintegrated. And I ceased hearing the harmonic, the patterned frequencies that transcend time and place. We will hear instead the bells as they are struck, in each moment.

VIII. Heaven and Earth

This now is the continual present, of yang heaven and yin earth, father and mother. My lovers all became steps I walked along a circle, tones I scaled upward until I found myself at the beginning again. My lover revolved until I could not predict his direction.

I will not meet him for months yet; we will not have these conversations for another year. I am in a dark place now, watching one man I love, as he loves someone else. I briefly contemplate how alone we all are, how this trigram is edged.

I will sit on a porch in early summer and tell him everything: about how I have always liked him, about his secret interest in another woman. "I do not want to be a part of this triangle," I say. I was in a triad years before.

I am at peace with this past which is also my future, that can remain in the present of duality, of binary couplings. He walks away continually, the *bagua* path open, center coiled in *taijitu*. That time is past, the ringing stopped; but stars carry on, regardless.

SOLO

an open letter

1

You enjoy music, hiking, cooking—and you enjoyed these things before you met me.

But you have never met me, nor anyone like me, and I suppose that's why we are alone.

Like me, you choose comfort over style most days, and sleep late when you can.

You are neat, but not fussy, and your nails are clean and trimmed.

When you began losing your hair, you shaved it off, or wore a hat, a bandanna.

Or, having a full mane, you opted for dreads, or keep it short these days, or put it up when you're working.

You enjoy working with words, wood, clay, iron, or earth. "Beautiful *and* functional," you say, smiling to yourself.

Form follows function. Everything you touch bends toward beauty and truth.

2

But you are frequently alone now, and talking only to yourself when you admire your work.

You don't drink much anymore (not that you ever enjoyed being drunk) and home is where you are most evenings.

Your friends are increasingly involved in their marriages, or with their children, and let's face it—you enjoy solitude better with each passing day.

You explain this to your sister or brother or mother or father, but the insistence that you *deserve to be happy* or that you need to *let go of the past* becomes the point of every conversation.

Or, no one asks how you're doing anymore, because they accept your loneliness as a feature of your personality, and would be concerned if your signature calm was broken by a wayward intrusion.

3

Wayward?

As if anything could ever be off course.

The impossibility of being diverted.

What direction does anything go but forward?

You watch the geese fly at their appropriate times, and recognize those times as markers in your life.

When was anything not on schedule?

Somewhere there is someone else who thinks these same thoughts.

A fatalist or a stoic.

A philosopher.

You turn back to your work, grateful that you can stop and begin, stop and begin.

Are you diverted?

Or on schedule?

Wayward has a nice sound.

You feel the itch to look it up, to know the etymology.

Surely an Anglo-Saxon word.

At the least, a word worth knowing the exact meaning of.

You favor exactitude, and have always liked knowing the meanings of things, their histories.

4

If I were there, I'd look the word up.

We would both take a break from our work and have a cup of tea.

We would speculate that we had been waywardly drawn toward this word, as if the path of our labor that day had been the right and only way, and any other, this brief digression, made us victims of a rebellious, errant urge.

To know something, to dwell—for just a moment—to be halted along the road that work and life maps out for us.

Even then, the paradox: is it possible to ever be diverted from one's journey, when the way one lives is the map itself?

Can we ever say that someone else pulls us away from the trajectory intended by our coordinate births?

5

But this is a solo, and you are not here with me and there is no hot tea or reason to be pulled from anything.

Every day there is only this one way to go, and I do not stop to wonder if I've misstepped.

I decide that given the way everything else has gone, there is only this road and no other.

I can't wonder if I shouldn't have gone to meet him, or if I could have known in advance how it would all turn out.

Mortal life brims with if onlys and muted instinct.

It was all wrong, the way it felt, but I didn't recognize the warning in my gut.

And soon I was in a moment where there were no clear choices, no freedom, none.

6

You weren't there when I spent that year trying to understand why.

You weren't there when I asked for water, and the man I was with said, "You'll just have to wait."

That night I lay in bed with him, resolving I'd been badly used, that I'd never see him again, and I didn't.

That night reminded me of another, over a year before, with a different man, when I had felt suffocated by his ambivalence and abandoned.

He'd said to me, perhaps half-dreaming, "Looking for a way out?"

An already sleepless night was made more restless after, as I tried to make sense of the question.

They might as well have been the same man, though I knew one for a short month, and the other a year.

7

I hear the original subject of every complaint; it is a wedge between me and every happiness that those in love—who stay in love—enjoy.

A burgeoning suspicion that I'm too quick or too slow, too far or too close, too in-between to ever get it right.

One toe in, but my arm firmly out.

Look over your shoulder, see me peering around my book, studying you:

How long this time?

How long until we change?

You reassure, prop my heart up with a gentle word.

When your back is turned, I inspect the scaffolding.

Is it you I mistrust, or my own futile faith?

You were never here when I needed you, so where are you now?

Now and tomorrow and last year.

You'll not survive this critique.

8

I tell myself that you have full lips and soft skin.

You are graceful with long, artistic fingers.

I almost believe in you.

You delight in the smell of smooth bourbon and Nag Champa, sweat, or fine cologne.

I like resting in your arms.

You burrow your face into my breasts.

I loosen the knot of fear a little more each day.

One day it disappears down the drain and I don't notice.

You stop asking me how I like my coffee and simply bring it.

You sit gently on my toes because you know they need warming, and pass me the paper you've already skimmed.

It's a Saturday and you're up early.

You won't speak your impatience but will wait politely.

It's market day and we're out of eggs.

9

Or, the reverse is true.

I go for a walk and you're already in the shower when I return.

I slide my slacks off and join you.

The morning is brisk, and the car's defroster is slow.

A deer grazes in the field by the bridge.

You talk me into muffins this time; last week it was the chocolate croissant.

Somehow after, the bookstore.

Just a minute, you say.

The eggs, I say.

They'll wait, you say.

I twist my mouth because I'm composing lines in my memory, and sip my coffee.

Fifteen minutes later, you return with three volumes, all first editions.

I gaze at the blur of mums near the turn by the post.

You chatter about Gurdjieff and I try to remember the essay I'd begun.

10

And you do—*chatter*, I mean.

I'm trying to think and you talk on, without realizing I'm glazing over, or somewhere else.

Your monologues become predictable, and I feign listening more often.

Faculty meetings help me refine my technique.

Smile and nod.

Take pencil in hand and jot notes.

Funny how much writing I begin when you think I'm pondering your best thoughts.

When I say I need to be alone for a short while—to work, I say—you appear hurt, but let me go.

If you knew how many times I sit staring at the screen, afraid to write the words I hear when you're talking.

Afraid that you'll comb my essays looking for evidence that my mind wanders away in the night.

That I'm only partly here.

11

The thoughts that haunt those who sail or fly alone:

I've stopped searching for you just as I've stopped waiting for myself, to come on time, to be anywhere worth being.

I stopped asking where you were when I found new sentences to fill your absence.

In the end we say absolutely nothing, in one mute voice together.

Solo, I wonder how much nothing costs, and whether it comes in blue.

I become a minimalist.

I forget where I put all of the things I don't need.

Soon, I am just a body and then not even that, moving through the world complete.

I've never needed you, I've never needed anything but silence and space.

Pure space that surrounds me no matter how much I try to give it away.

12

You might say there are intervals between us, of times spent with this or that lover, and that we fail to be more than isolate parallels.

One of us is alone, the other inopportunely mated.

Time stops and moves retrograde for a season.

We betray or are betrayed, and roles shift.

You are that lover I see across the room, but the script is wrong.

Your eyes catch mine, just as someone hands you your glass.

Your attention shifts, lighting on the one who laughs, gracefully sipping red wine.

You belong and I don't.

I'm the puzzle piece that falls from the table's edge.

You'll find me again in three years' time, but I'll be lost in the fantasy of a potential lover, too young.

The affair will be short-lived.

13

Funny—you argue that neither of us ever really transgressed enough.

They were not nearly so young as we imagine them to have been.

(Better, they don't exist at all. I made them up, a comfort on a cold October night.)

You never really suffered overly long for the lover who now brings wine to someone (not you) at another party in a distant city.

In fact, they were never ours, though they appeared so.

A year passes, then five more.

We are older tonight than we were when we didn't meet a decade ago.

I can make up ex-lovers and near-misses unceasing; I have a full bottle of whiskey in the cabinet.

Not that I ever drank to fill the void of your absence . . . still.

14

I'll sit in the café or the park, waiting for that second chance meeting.

Every luncheon with friends, I'll steal a glimpse at the other table, hoping to see you turn to face me, surprised by our accidental reunion.

There you are.

We'll be familiar, but strange.

You won't recognize me, these days.

I'm a woman or I'm a man—what's the difference?

I have silver hair or it's brown, long enough for me to pull back, or it's gone altogether.

Let's skip the histrionics; we're quite old, and it would be beyond our powers to escape the solitudes we've found through time.

Only remembering makes sense, and our coupling would be laughable.

I am the grandparent who never remarried.

I am both of them.

You were never mine.

15

It's early (or late, depending), and you caught me in a dream.

In it, you and I were lovers, then we were strangers who never became lovers, and then we were old and had forgotten that we had been lovers.

When my students write their dreams into essays, they shift into the present tense, unconsciously.

I am similarly lost in time, and you console me with your touch, ever the second person in the bed, ever the "you" that I feared never knowing, then forgot.

It doesn't matter that this is an illusion: your hands, your body, your lips on my face, your moans when we close the distance between our pleasures.

We've grounded our arrivals and departures. I feel guilty sometimes for doubting you, for doubting that you exist.

16

Still, it's possible to run out of faces: the face I wear for you when I'm only partially paying attention, or the face that says I'm not really fine, and I need you to hold me.

There's one for all the things you'll never know, because at some age, we stop telling our lovers everything.

You'll never get entirely inside my head.

It's good that we didn't know each other when.

There are no irrelevancies, I swear this has all been planned.

Not only that, but I've already been here.

I put the coat back into the closet, lock the door.

I'm not coming to meet you.

I'm not leaving.

I don't know who you are.

It's all been forgotten, and I simply don't recall.

The time tangles free, undone.

CIRCLE OF FIFTHS

Lessons in Syntax

INSTRUCTIONS: Compose or complete the sentences expressed by the following diagrams, fill in the missing elements of the partial diagrams, or create new diagrams for the sentences provided. You may use a separate sheet of paper.

I. The Runaway

1. When my grandmother died that summer, I knew
   _____ .

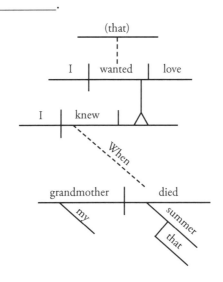

2. I drove back from the beach the day before her funeral, met my friends, got drunk, and went to a concert.
3. My friends worried when I left my purse and phone under my chair and disappeared into the July night to weep.
4. I also wept because the man I loved _____.

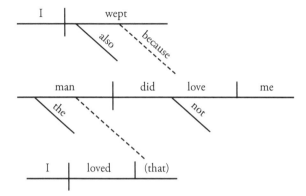

5. My grandmother's funeral was attended by family, friends, her
   ex-husband, grandchildren, my father's mother, and
   _____.

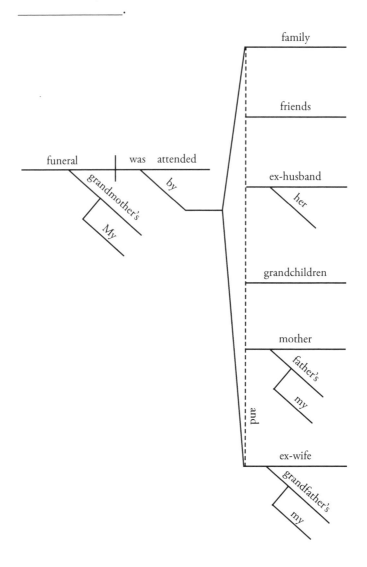

6. My uncle pointed to _____ on her casket and called them snowbirds.

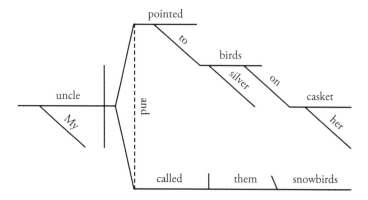

7. My grandmother used to tell a story about a young girl who runs away from home after getting in trouble for fighting with her brother.

8. A storm comes; she hides under a _____, falls asleep, and is awakened by a _____.

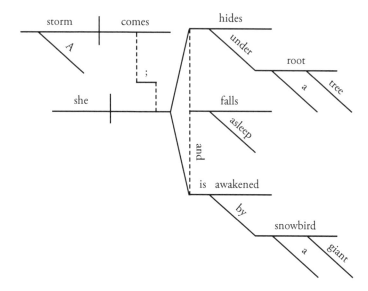

9. The snowbird flies her to a place _____ where _____ creatures know her by name.

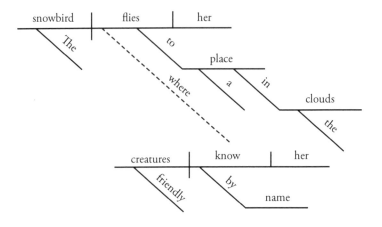

10. The girl becomes homesick, and the snowbird weeps a tear that turns into a pearl when she says she wants to go home.

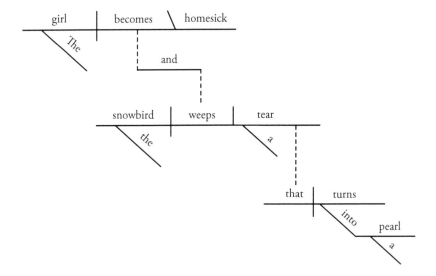

11. The girl finds the pearl in her pocket when she is embraced by her distraught mother, and she promises never to run away again.

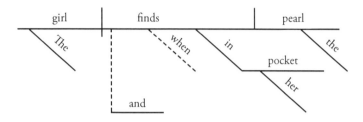

12. The preacher sang the song my grandmother loved while I stared at the snowbirds on the casket.

II. A Shift in Orbit

1. After my grandmother's funeral, _____ I joined a popular dating website.

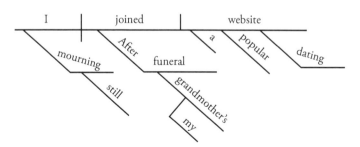

2. Within minutes, my profile was viewed by the man I loved, who immediately blocked me from contacting him.

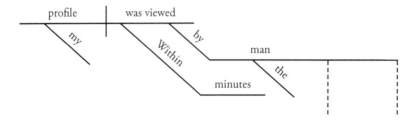

3. This impersonal rejection from a friend was too much to bear.
4. Later I mentioned that I had seen him _____.

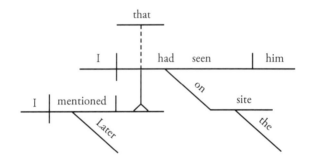

5. I realized I belonged to a category of persons not overlapping with his Venn diagrams of potential romantic partners.

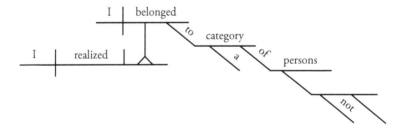

6. What had been opaque was finally clear.
7. For two weeks, I sifted through dating profiles.

8. Disappointed and finished with trying, I logged onto a different site to close an old profile.

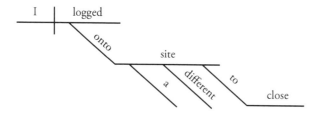

9. Before _____, a man had emailed me _____ and he was _____.

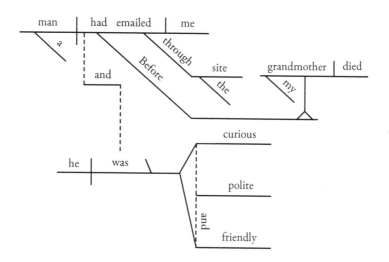

10. I was surprised when we began to correspond and my _____ shifted.

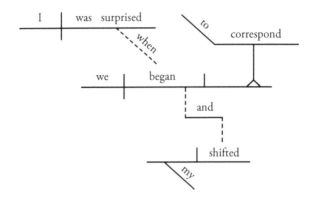

11. We emailed one another after that for weeks, about our children, _____, our common interests.

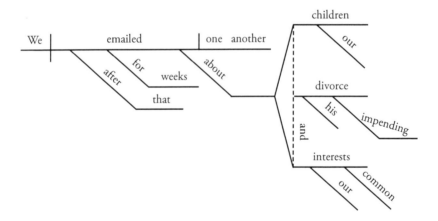

12. The timing of his entry into my life was never insignificant.

III. Rings

1. When we first met he gave me a _____ and called it a token.

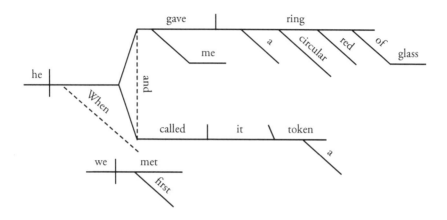

2. I still _____ and sometimes admire its smooth, burgundy form.

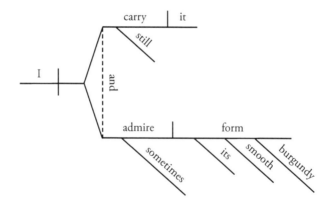

3. We sometimes spend _____, where his wife still lives, until she _____ and moves out.

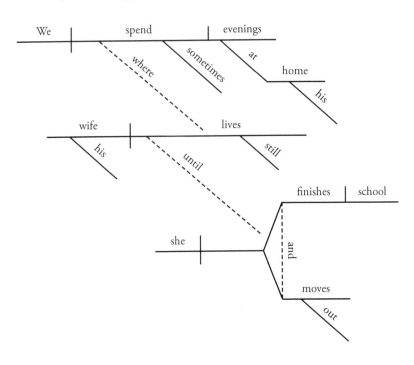

4. Our children play _____ our families are together.

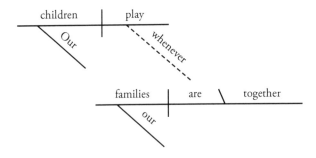

5. _____, their mother's girlfriend drives up for the weekend.

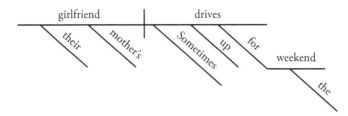

6. After the children are _____, my boyfriend, _____, her lover, and I _____ and drink.

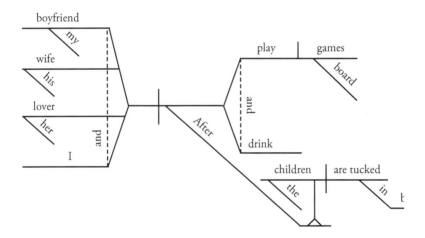

7. Sometimes we laugh loud, and worry about waking the kids.

8. My boyfriend and _____ had wanted _____ and nights like these.

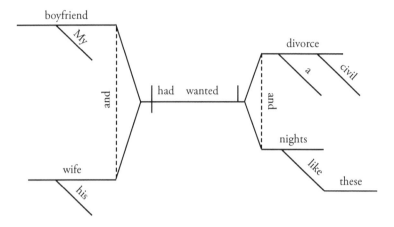

9. The arrangement is hard to explain to others, yet the children love these extra parents they have gained.

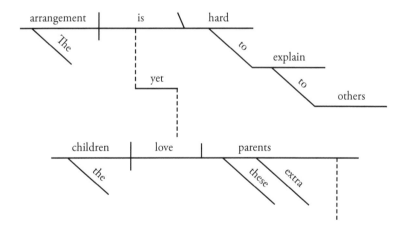

10. Notes and drawings on my fridge show that I am a part of their life.
11. I do not think my son is ready for siblings.
12. When we are at home on lonely nights, I sympathize with him while washing a single sink of dishes.

IV. Cul-de-sac

1. My _____ lives an hour away, and as I drive, I
think about the circles we create.

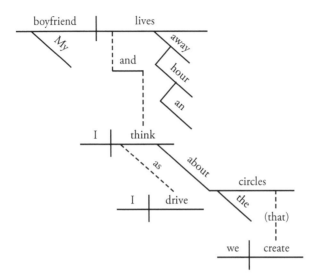

2. I drove _____ every week to see _____
and hear her _____ goodbyes.

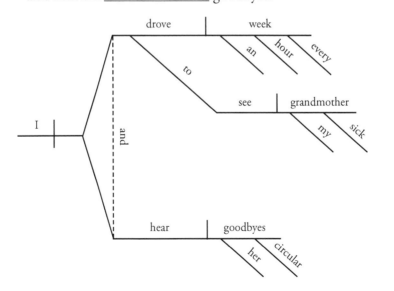

3. "If you don't go, you can't come back."
4. Our first date, my boyfriend and I went to the bar I had visited before my grandmother's funeral.
5. In that bar the night before her funeral, I drank far too much, and began to cry.
6. Sometimes I feel my grandmother's presence and I think about her every day.

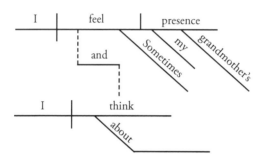

7. My grandmother and I loved to talk late into the night about the complex patterns people create with one another, the circles that bring them together.
8. My grandfather visited her _____ before her death though they were _____ .

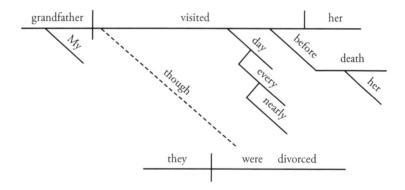

9. My grandfather's children from _____ loved and
    respected my grandmother.

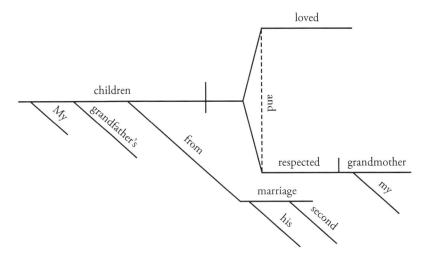

10. I learned about alternative family structures by watching my
    own blocked lanes, their crossings and recrossings.

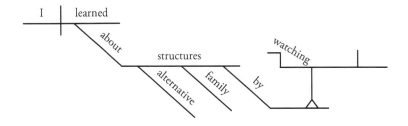

11. My mother and grandmother had lived in marriages shaped
    like cul-de-sacs.
12. Because of this, I understand how men and women can mire
    themselves together.

V. Root Chords

1. Perhaps the lines that tie us all to each other are lines of fate.
2. We do not need the bonds of family to be fixed in relational webs.
3. The mapping of hearts is not linear but circular, though measures are effectively both.
4. A piece of music advances through play that can stop and begin again from different points.
5. All lines circle back to _____.

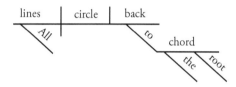

6. I have never known where a sentence was going before I wrote it, even though I hear subjects and phrases at the outset.
7. Relationships similarly speak to me as sentences, impossible to diagram without losing the pacing, the order, the sound of them.
8. Instead, we see merely the logic of notation, a skeletal heap.
9. Prose inters the thoughts I wish to hold, beyond their own usefulness.
10. What any of us do with these words will forever divide us, and even so, we have not met under ideal conditions.

II. _____ under ideal conditions.

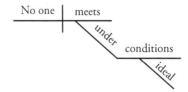

12. This knowing _____.

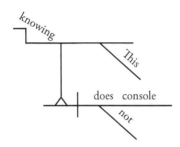

INTERVALS

I.

In late February my lover explains the nature of his twenty-year-long friendship with a woman he's known since college. Theirs is an intimate friendship, and I know that he talks about our relationship with her, when they meet up to drink together, or spend time in her art studio. She is married, but has recently expressed thoughts about divorcing, which my lover supports. "I don't think they are right for each other," he says, and I bristle, grateful that he and I are on the phone, that he can't see my reaction. Later, I mention that I am uncomfortable with him spending such a long drunken evening with her. I'm jealous, I admit, and though I know it to be a fault, I don't think I can handle these feelings alone. He points out that jealousy arises from insecurity, and I counter that jealousy is a clarifier—that it shows me we have been unclear about what we are to each other. I suddenly want to know if we are exclusive with one another, or if he has been imagining us otherwise, perhaps polyamorous.

I know him to be radical in his thinking about sex. After all, he is still married, though divorcing, and his wife still lives with him. She takes long weekends to visit her girlfriend in another city, three hours away, leaving their two children in his care. We walk through the forest on a cold winter day, and my hands are frozen in my pockets. The children begin to complain that they are cold too, and I realize other parts of me—my heart, my mind—are slowing and becoming colder as we converse, voices lowered when the kids catch up to us on our long hike along a windy river. Normally, I look forward to these walks, because his children fight less and the dogs are given the chance to run free of leashes. Sometimes on warm days we have lain in the grass and talked while the children climbed low-hanging branches, and once, my own son joined us for a walk that became hours of harmonious imaginative play for him and my lover's two children; they are all nearly the same age.

During these beatific interludes, I often fantasize our companionship into something more solid. The month before, I traded my functional four-seater for a car that could accommodate five. His two children and my one are additional reasons for our compatibility. My lover and I are the same age, and past believing that marriage is an outcome for every strong bond. We are content to live in our separate cities and houses one hour away, and alternate driving over a mountain weekly, sometimes biweekly, in order to be together. Sometimes he brings the children and the dogs. Sometimes it's just him. Often I leave work early to be there on Friday, returning on Sunday morning. Sometimes my child is with me. Rarely are we alone. I think about this on an evening when we sit together in my kitchen. It is late, and my son is asleep. It's a school night, and I will be tired all day tomorrow. But my lover explains that he and his female friend sometimes "snuggle," and sex is a mysterious event that could overtake them, though it never has.

II.

While researching intervals I find schematas for identifying musical keys with emotions, or colors, from different centuries.[14] Other websites lead me to words I haven't used since my ninth-grade class in music theory: major, minor, scale, tone, tonic, tonality. Bass teacher Andrew Pouska describes "key" on his webpage resource, StudyBass:

> When you play music, the music is constantly being pulled toward the tonic, or root of the key, wanting to come to a state of rest or completion. The tonic is the most resolved note in a key. *The tonic*

is a key's center. . . . Moving away from and back to the tonic resting
point of the key is partly what makes music interesting and why it
has a pleasing effect on us. Continuing the gravity analogy, music
momentarily defies gravity, but then comes back down.[15]

My relationship with my lover is like that, only gravity does not
bring me back to a place of security, but one of doubt. Our conversations are euphoric and wild; when I am alone, I try to unravel the
knot of his revolutionary logic.

A few days later, we lie in bed, and I'm trying not to cry. I want to
know what "snuggle" means because I do not snuggle with anyone
but him, and I say this with emphasis, adding a list of things that I
only do with him, and no one else. Apparently, I had overreacted; by
snuggle, he meant a comforting embrace. Perhaps sitting close on
a couch together, but not making out, as I had fully imagined. We
talk more, specifically about how he defines polyamory. Based on
the numerous books about human sexuality he's consumed over the
years, he says, it's just about making space for one another to be who
we are naturally with other people. We may have any number of
intense friendships apart from our relationship, but we respect the
other's freedom to define those relationships, which are not always
sexual. And perhaps, he speculates, one of those friendships may become sexual, but we do not necessarily seek those out. Instead, we
focus on one another's happiness and permit each other the freedom
to be who we really are.

I type these words hesitantly, and realize they made better sense
when I was lying beside him. Tonight, home with my son and an
hour away, I wait ten, twenty, thirty minutes for him to text me
back. I asked "How was your day?" but what I really meant was
"Are you with her tonight?" Despite his assertion that he would "do
nothing to jeopardize our relationship," I feel us to be in jeopardy
now. Whatever thoughts I had before are gone and replaced by this
searing jealousy. I keep thinking about something else he had told
me, after I'd almost relaxed again into believing everything was settled between us. She had shown him her breasts the last time they
were together. After her double mastectomy, she feared her husband
was no longer attracted to her. So, seeking validation perhaps, or at
the least, some kind of response, she bared her implanted breasts.

He describes their scars as startling, but I don't see them so in my mind. Instead, they are *firm,* the way he had described them weeks before in a passing comment.

III.

Though I can see designs all around me in so many things, I rarely recognize the destructive patterns in my romantic life. My persistent error has always been that I believe in my own interpretations of reality, and am frequently wrong. Love is blind, but I add that I am deaf and dumb, not hearing the dissonances early enough, and unable to speak my worries aloud for fear that I'll offend. For now, I may retreat into an essay on music theory, and leave the rest for later working out. (Still, I wait for a word from him and time lengthens.) I look over my notes on "tritones," a musical interval of three adjacent tones once considered dissonant and even "dangerous," but later essential to the study of musical harmony, beginning with the Baroque period. I run across the term *diabolus in musica,* and the idea that evil lurks in certain chords or intervals with a dissonant quality. Intrigued, I read about the Counter-Reformation, and The Council of Trent (1562 CE), which, among other things, banished organs, professional musicians, and polyphonic singing from cloisters.

Difficult to imagine the loss of multiple voices in a piece of music, or the working out of harmonies, and even harder the loss of these from all music meant to glorify God. I read elsewhere that claims of a ban on polyphonic singing are apocryphal, and there is no evidence for this assertion. Even so, The Council of Trent did other things to counter the revolutionary ideas sweeping Europe, such as establish that those who divorce can never remarry, so long as the ex-spouse is still alive, even if the other had committed adultery. I find so many things troubling about religion, generally, including this particular matter of divorce. Though I am not Catholic, or even Christian for that matter, I live with the cultural baggage of centuries, and a hankering for stability. Although I have by now accepted the possibility of never remarrying, I rankle at the thought of being barred from it. What's more, I consider the required celibacy of clergy to be somewhat relevant to the sexual abuses in the Catholic Church. Repression, denial, guilt—where has it gotten us?

My lover texts back, having been engaged in all the typical things for him that bring him joy: practicing his martial art, walking the dogs along the river, preparing dinner. I'm regretful that I had allowed my mind to swarm with images that don't fit the reality. He is loving, kind—the man I've come to believe in most. I'm sure his friendship is a comfort to the woman whose breasts I obsess over, and I try to imagine having lost so much to cancer. Recalling my own marriage, I remember the first time a man other than my husband touched my breasts, at that time filled with milk. For those few moments I felt beautiful again. It wasn't long before my divorce was underway. I wonder if my lover's friend seeks that feeling through him, and how far he would go to prove her beauty, and how lovely she is to him. Having met her twice, I try to reconcile what I know with what I don't know. She is gentle, outgoing, warm, and generous. All of us have needed such a friend.

IV.

I turn back to my study of tritones—the augmented fourth, the diminished fifth—unstable intervals that are the inverse of one another, but whose sum is one perfect octave. I read that the tritone pushes toward resolution, the augmented fourth resolving outward to minor or major sixth. The inverse may resolve, inwardly, to a major or minor third. My limited command of music is overtaken by a badly remembered study of music theory. I study the harmony of a third or a sixth, and can rapidly access these sounds should I want to hear them. I suppose the question becomes, which tone will move? And why can't we stop in the tritone and be content? Why the unsettled feeling? Returning to the historical mistrust of this interval, how does tonal resolution cohere with ideas of social stability, and is this too far a leap? Could some relationships between people be intervals desirous of slippage into resolution? In English we sometimes quip that certain things or people "strike a chord" with us, and I wonder what chord we mean, and what chords won't do.

The first time my lover and I discussed polyamory, I felt an excitement typically reserved for taboo ideas. I would be lying if I said his words didn't resonate with me, though I hesitate to identify the extent of my sympathies. Days later, I think of the tritone, the unsettled interval forming a chord that wants to settle into something else. I imagine one of us as the unsettled tone, perhaps seeking the third or sixth, a comfort provided by being in concert with one another, in a harmony we both hear and understand. *But which of us will move?* Am I more of a monoamorist than I'd previously imagined? If I attempted polyamory, would I eventually be led into another interval, even further away from the man I claim to love? The complication comes in different degrees and scales, and the tones scramble until I hear a cacophony of disordered attempts to find harmony or resolution in the unsettled intervals of past error. What then, lover? My faith in improvisation travels only so far before I seek something more solid and masterfully resolved.

Two days pass and I am tormented by breasts. I am ashamed to admit to this now, but they have become the augmented fourth of every hour, sounding like a steeple song to punctuate the breaks I take in reading and teaching, the thoughts I have in my car. I am driven mad by wondering. A quick text to him signals that I'm upset, and he calls me that night. At first I passionately assert my discomfort with where we are, and my unreadiness to think of all the relationships we are in with other people as more than simple friendships. Once again I am soothed by his admission that we may not be at that place yet where more sexualized feelings can come into play with those we interact with daily, apart from one another. He loves me, this I'm sure of, and he is supportive of our ability to even talk about what for him is still nearly as new for him as it is for me. And of his friend? She does not intend to replace me. Somehow I believe him.

V.

The next day I do not worry, but instead notice the ways I interact with others around me at work. A male colleague and fellow writer sits working on the typography for the journal we edit for; I laugh with him over a shared remark, that the cover of the journal, a smoke plume, resembles a vagina. The previous day, several of us had chided him on his Rorschach vision. "That's one messed up clitoris," I had said. This morning, when I touch his shoulder, the gesture is natural and unfettered by misunderstanding. As I walk back to my office I realize that I often touch people without thinking, never meaning anything more than camaraderie. Later, a student asks me how I'm doing, and I say, "Much better than yesterday." We had talked about my concerns over polyamory, and he had sympathized with me, *worried* with me, over the complexity of such things, expressed his own leanings toward monoamory with the men he loves, though there are those uncommitted relationships he's managed in concurrent waves. He pulls me into an embrace, to comfort me.

Another student listens while I analyze threads in his essay-in-progress, and we're talking about the precipice of adulthood, the yawning chasm of nihilism that threatens with the possibility of there being no God, thus no order to things. I point out markers of his fear and moments of his personal life in the essay, and observe how he takes it all in, how easily we talk about things that most people never confront with anyone other than their closest friends. After holiday breaks and during celebrations, I have hugged him, and if I were to give an accounting, I'd say that most of my students have reached for me as someone who appreciates humanity. I don't think there has ever been confusion over meaning. And yet, there are some people so obsessed with sex as the primary motivator behind human relationships, that they would criticize or misalign such attention, and warn me to be more distant. I do not deny that there are attractions between students and teachers; even so, mine remain transparent, have always been. I recognize the harmonious intervals of my profession.

A female colleague and I walk to our cars, discussing a married friend of hers who is in love with her fitness instructor. She and her husband are trying to work through her attraction, but nothing short of an affair seems possible. I touch my friend's arm in farewell and am aware of it, and suddenly cognizant of how radiant she is. We realize that we should get together for lunch sometime since we both want to talk more about this, as she doesn't know what to tell her friend that will make sense. On the way home, I call my aunt, who has always been a mother to me. Her colonoscopy was clear she says, but she's never going through that again. She makes a crudely outrageous remark that makes me chortle, and I think about how close we are, that we can share this humor. And yet, I know that I may never tell her about where my relationship is going. Some things have already become impossible to share with anyone but my lover. This thought chides, but I'm still only midway.

VI.

For the second night in a row, my lover calls me. Generally we don't talk on the phone but perhaps once a week, if that. I'm aware that he's reaching for me now, bothered over matters at work, and whether he has the gas money to make it over the mountain to see me that week. I reassure him, and we talk aimlessly at first, then move steadily into matters more dear. He asks me a question I've been afraid to answer for several months now: Who, among my friends, am I most attracted to sexually? He catches my avoidance and calls me out. When I finally explain, I wonder how much I'm still not saying: I had been in love with someone before him, and I still interact with this person among my social circles, though we share a tense estrangement. I relate as much as I can about the ways I used to believe that we had used music to communicate secret feelings neither he nor I could ever have for each other, though I eventually discovered his involvement with someone else.

Surprisingly, my lover patiently listens, and says it is possible that this other man and I might continue on in this way for many years, and that it is likely that we will remain divided by our responsibilities, our reasons for not being able to pursue a romantic relationship, but still seek one another through other means. Without my lover's saying so, I understand that being in a committed relationship with him is not an impediment to exploration with others. Tables turned, my hypocrisy apparent (though perhaps only to me), I nervously laugh over the idea that I could be intimate with anyone other than him. I hear myself asserting that I am fulfilled by him, and desire no second. The irony disturbs me some, that even with such liberty and frankness, I cannot easily imagine desiring anyone else. In fact, straying seems impossible in the face of so much honesty. He has only to call me to him, and I am like a hound, hungry for his affection. Such openness has never been mine before, and I'm disarmed by his generosity; its audacity.

In darker moments, I look for signs that we are merely shearing attachments, preparing for eventual erosion into a friendship only slightly complicated by our mutual attraction. Perhaps we will not have so many more days together then, as they gently become weeks. Another day by the river, this one every bit as cold as previous times, we wait by the river's edge while the children clamber down a bank newly calved from the trail. The silty earth has dropped into the river creating a slope, and while my lover cuts the brambles obstructing the children's new playground, I watch him thoughtfully. This day we talk less, and I think more, keeping so much to myself. He doesn't push me to account for my silence. There is far too much to mull over, and I walk on by myself for a while to warm up before turning back. The river evolves, the ground becomes saturated, then drains again. The children have found a fallen tree. When I return, I thread my arm through my lover's and we stand that way for a long time.

GAME THEORY

Fold into the shape of an origami fortune teller. Spell letters of capped letters to begin game. (Example: SCHOLAR has seven letters, so open and close the fortune teller in the direction of arrows until you have spelled out the word, which is seven times.) Choose an adjective and spell it to count, while opening and closing. Select a word and look under the flap to find the noun, as well as the phrase that completes the sentence.

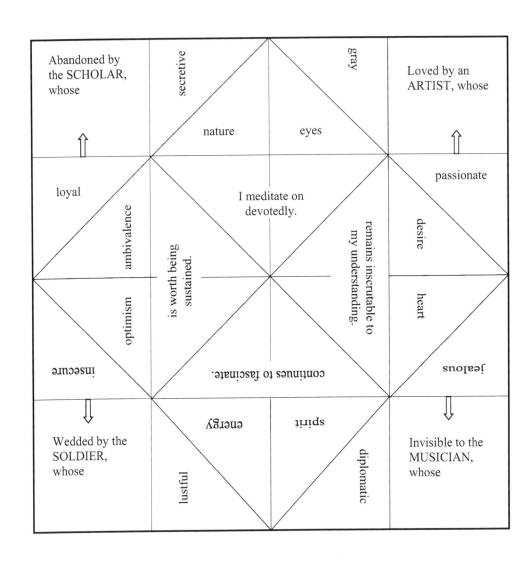

RITE OF MIRRORS

Philosopher and essayist Michel de Montaigne once surmised that obsession is the wellspring of genius and madness.[16] Can we say this of art, generally? In the spring of my thirty-eighth year, at the same age Montaigne was when he retired to write his essays, I became obsessed with twentieth-century composer Igor Stravinsky. Stravinsky composed the controversial *Rite of Spring*, which premiered in 1913; the ballet, based on Russian folk stories and songs, caused an uproar of historic proportions. The police were called because the Paris audience began rioting, in a fury because the music was so freakishly dissonant, and because the ballet was choreographed by Nijinsky in ways some considered lewd.

What the audience saw that night in 1913 was unlike any ballet they had seen before. Billowy and delicate tutus were replaced by sack-like peasant garments and garish makeup. Convulsive throbbing took the place of graceful leaping. The lights in the Théâtre des Champs-Élysées flashed on and off, on and off, in an attempt to reestablish order. The chaos of that evening gestured toward the looming horror of World War I, which began less than a year later and crippled all of Europe in its aftermath. It is difficult to not hear the impending devastation, and recognize something hauntingly prophetic in this piece of music, the sacrificial rite ushering spring's violent return.

My thirty-eighth spring I was intently reading Stravinsky's *Poet-ics of Music,* a series of lectures he gave at Harvard in 1939 and 1940, and I was finding that much of what he said about music composi-tion could also be applied to essays. Mine was a cerebral love, an ob-sessive orbit around Stravinsky and his music, and I listened to his *Rite of Spring,* known in French as *Le Sacre du printemps,* repeatedly, for days, stretching into weeks, coming to hear music where most of my life before I'd heard only jumbled notes. Hearing music instead of noise after two decades of listening was pure epiphany, an awak-ening to new orders and patterns.

Imagine my delight when I also discovered a 2009 French film about Igor Stravinsky's alleged love affair with the iconic fashion designer Coco Chanel. The film was directed by Jan Kounen, star-ring Anna Mouglalis and Mads Mikkelsen as Chanel and Stravin-sky. The film began with the earth-shattering premiere of *The Rite of Spring,* recreating it faithfully. Watching, I felt as if I had been there, amid all of the post-Edwardian decadence, at the exact mo-ment when the boos and catcalls escalated into cacophony, as the dancers sweated and furiously throttled themselves forward despite the jeering crowd. Nijinsky bellowed the count for his dancers from the wings, as the music was drowned out.

The story that takes place during the majority of the film centers on several months in 1920, when Igor Stravinsky, his sickly wife, and their children moved into Chanel's country estate. He was finan-cially destitute and Chanel offered to support him and his family so that he could continue composing. It was not unusual in Europe during that time for wealthy patrons to support the arts. Still, some-times there were relationships behind the gifts, and this story makes the most of tenuous conjecture. The self-sufficient Chanel support-ing a humbled Stravinsky presents a tempting twist on the oldest dependency that men and women can have for one another. Her generosity empowers erotic suggestion.

Chanel was fiercely independent with her sexuality and Stravin-sky was married to a woman with tuberculosis. Aside from this, it is true that Chanel and Stravinsky were friends. He gave her a valu-able Russian icon that still sits on a bookshelf behind her writing desk at 31 Rue Cambon in the apartment above her Paris boutique. She anonymously funded a revival of *The Rite of Spring* by the Ballet

Russes in late 1920. Whether or not they were lovers is a possibility that the film explores with gusto. That these two artists, the designer and the musician, both composers of sorts, could inspire one another's work, forms the mystery behind the film.

Stravinsky's music changed after 1920, the year he lived with Chanel, becoming less focused on narrative and more about allowing the music itself to build coherence. Chanel No. 5 was created in 1920 as well, after Chanel chose the scent her perfumer offered among ten vials known only by number. Chanel spent her early life in a convent, and paths leading to the cathedral were designed in circular patterns repeating the number five. She released her collections on the fifth day of the fifth month, so for her, number five was the right scent and the right name for the perfume that is her legacy, bearing a number she considered personally significant.

As a writer, I am taken aback by these correspondences, just as I am sure author Chris Greenhalgh was when he took on the project that evolved into the 2002 semi-biographical novel *Coco & Igor* upon which the film is based. Writers look for the ways patterns emerge in life, naturally unfolding from historic or imagined events. The relationships that are embedded in these designs become the scaffolding and inspiration for stories. I don't write fiction, but sometimes I wish I did. My own life provides the stories and patterns my craft responds to. I essay connections between what I learn and consume, what I observe and reflect on when I'm alone.

Numbers hold great significance for me, and more than once I have compulsively restrained myself to word counts and prose structures simply because I've craved the order that numbers provide. Although I am poor at math, I am attracted to the stability a number or formula provides. I am likewise no musician, but have found in my studies of music theory countless examples of composers building numerological patterns into their compositions, even to the point that dissertations are written about them, and new stories emerge in the wake of what we know to be too uncanny to be merely accidental. Relationships between harmonies and melodies overtake the dramas of the merely human.

The same spring I studied Chanel and Stravinsky, I was also in the midst of a deteriorating relationship with a man whom I'd been in love with for nearly six months, who, with very little warning, decided that he was polyamorous. He thought we should date other people, and argued that several intimate friendships are better than just one. This radical plan for our relationship ran counter to everything I believed, and I struggled with the idea. It felt wrong to me, though I could see his point, some of the time, that human beings may not be monogamous by nature, though we certainly tend to be outwardly singular in our affections.

If you are unfortunate enough to be in love with someone who cannot love you back completely, it is altogether too easy to convince yourself that becoming what the other person wants will earn you the love you desire. It was this way for me, and in hindsight, I wonder how I could have been so foolish. The film, *Coco Chanel and Igor Stravinsky,* served as an intellectual distraction for a while. I focused on these characters, distant reflections of my own life, and made notes about the film compulsively, watching it repeatedly to get everything recorded just right, uncovering the most fascinating details about the film through my single-minded, obsessive attention.

Even though it was chosen as the closing film of the 2009 Cannes Film Festival, it wasn't particularly lauded with accolades. In fact, most of the film's reviews are critical of the intimacy between the lovers, and the detached way their hypothetical affair is rendered and executed. After watching it more than six times, and taking over fifty screenshots to analyze later, I wondered how anyone could have missed the film's conceptual brilliance. There are multiple symbolic gestures, which lead us to see Chanel and Stravinsky's romantic relationship as inevitable, but fraught with egoism, vanity, and selfishness. There are at least fifty-six mirrors or instances of mirroring and reflections in this film.

My interest in Stravinsky and his *Poetics of Music* emerged from research I was doing for a book I'd begun the previous year, based on Johannes Sebastian Bach's *The Art of Fugue*, a masterwork of fourteen fugues that plays with the development and reworking of a single musical subject, or melody, into fourteen different permutations. I intended to write an essay for each of the corresponding fugues in Bach's *Art of Fugue*, with each essay mimicking either the form or some other arcane aspect of each fugue in my prose. Just as Bach himself had played with numerical puzzles and created riddles in his compositions, I did the same in my essays.

It was complete fixation on my part, and a friend characterized this kind of writing behavior as schizophrenic. I won't argue with that assessment, though I would add that obsessive-compulsive behavior is something less troubling than schizophrenia, and fairly commonplace among writers. And yet, I tried to model my work on that of a genius, and there's something deeply disturbing about such an impossible exercise. Nothing is more humbling than limiting an essay to a certain number of paragraphs, each paragraph built with only a precise number of words, or, in one extreme instance, making words stand in for rests and notes in an attempt to replicate a piece of sheet music.

It's a game, really, once you go down that path as an artist, like trying to recreate all of Van Gogh's paintings in miniature on napkins, using only three colors and a rabbit's foot instead of a paintbrush. Nothing is so ludicrous than the idea that you will make art under such circumstances, and nothing is so surprising as your own willingness to submit to such a challenge. Have you ever loved anything or someone so much that you would deform yourself into something unrecognizable? I have, and in so many ways and contexts that it would be disingenuous to pretend I have been more than a refraction of those past instances.

I was at that point in my writing project where I had only a few more essays to complete, and Bach's cleverness had become a monumental conceit—one that I paid for, frequently line-by-line. Two of the fugues in *The Art of Fugue* are "mirror fugues." That is, they are compositions which mirror one another exactly, but by inverting the four voices which make up the fugue itself. The bass from the first fugue becomes the soprano in the mirror, tenor becomes alto, alto becomes tenor, soprano becomes bass. And it's still musical, even beautiful. How was I going to accomplish this mirroring in prose, without literally repeating whole passages in reverse?

Uncannily, the moment after I counted the number of mirrors and reflective instances in the film about Stravinsky and Chanel, I discovered there were fifty-six, the same number of measures as in the first mirror fugue by Bach. So what if my lover wanted to date every woman and man in his town simultaneously? I had been blessed with the most perfect setup for an essay I'd ever encountered. And best of all, I was the only person writing about the film who saw these correspondences. In other ways, the relationship between Chanel and Stravinsky highlighted my romantic confusion. I wondered whether I sympathized with Chanel's freedom, or with Stravinsky's devoted wife.

Infidelity has always troubled me, because I was once married to someone who continually tested my patience. I tried to be an understanding wife, despite his repetitive dalliances: female hiking companions and drinking buddies he met up with after class, and the last spontaneous distraction of our marriage—the grad student he made out with by a campfire, even as I cared for our toddler at home. Over the years, friends told stories far worse, about a husband who had several secret affairs over the course of their marriage, or another man, who told his girlfriend he didn't find her attractive anymore, only hours after she had given birth to his child.

We may consider these men selfish, egotistical, perhaps even narcissistic. In the Greek myth which inspires such a reading, Narcissus spurns Echo, who loved him absolutely. She wasted away, cursed to repeat only what others said, while he ignored her, in rapture over his own reflection. People with narcissistic personalities are concerned only with their own needs, and see the people they are involved with as fuel for their own egos. Partners are replaceable, and commitment is conditionally given or revoked, since narcissists will rarely (if ever) make sacrifices for the happiness of others. Some affairs could be read as narcissistic, when selfish pleasure is primary to every other expression of love.

: :

So it was spring, exactly one hundred years after Igor Stravinsky's *Rite of Spring* premiered in Paris, and I was preoccupied with the dissonance in my own life at the same time that I was watching *Coco Chanel and Igor Stravinsky*, a story quite possibly about two narcissists falling in love. Thus began my self-interrogation: what is love, but a moment when I see myself reflected in the visage of someone else? Isn't narcissism the love of one's own reflection, however it appears? And what to make of a film that was widely considered a failure, but so richly layered with questions about art and life? Perhaps irony is a reflective pool?

A *New York Times* reviewer said the film portrayed "the selfish competitive passion of egomaniacal geniuses locked in erotic combat" but asserted that it deviated into a "wishy-washy ending."[17] I wondered—how could it not? The trajectory of a love affair with a narcissist typically runs the same course. The first few months are euphoric, blissful, perfect. And finally, as the narcissist becomes disenchanted and restless for variety, the relationship plummets. The magic of the romance fades into cold reality, egoism overtakes mutuality, and there might be a momentary appeal to old attachments and dependencies, with no result. Whether the relationship explodes or whispers, it damages the one who gave the most.

When one person sacrifices him or herself at the altar of the selfish, the narcissist moves easily on, indifferent. What happens when the relationship itself is narcissistic, having its genesis in obsession and lust? If you watch *Coco Chanel and Igor Stravinsky* with any attention at all, you'll see two narcissists locked in the gaze of themselves reflected in the mirror of the other's ego. And after the moment whereby they confront themselves as utterly self-involved individuals, the romance dissolves into dissonance, every bit as exactingly frenetic as Stravinsky's *Rite of Spring*. Such loss is sometimes a brutal sacrifice, but one that results in transformation of the creative process and one's art.

Occasionally, things that are perfectly obvious to me are not obvious to anyone else. And sometimes, what is obvious to others is completely opaque to me. Such was the case with my polyamorous lover. Every friend and relative tried to reason with me. But I believed that I loved him. More accurately, I saw something about myself in him, and was captured by its glittering sameness, before realizing how different we were later. I tend to immerse myself too rapidly, too eagerly, while feigning freedom, more so if the object of my affections is safely distant. Perhaps he wasn't everything I'd hoped for either, and sensing my doubts, he hedged his bets.

If we're being compassionate to this admission, and I hope we try to be when judging others, he had probably seen aspects in me that pleased him because they reminded him of himself. A sculptor and a martial artist, he claimed that relationships had become his life's medium. How can two artists, no matter the mediums, not find the ways their arts intersect, when there's attraction between them impossible to ignore? I have digressed far from the subject of mirrors and Bach's fugues. This essay I'm writing now is far away from the essay I intended to write months ago, when I still thought he and I had many years before us.

: :

When I watch *Coco Chanel and Igor Stravinsky*, a film that I eventually bought because I couldn't keep it rented out forever, I see fragments of the greater mirror between art and life. Stravinsky looks into mirrors, his hands are reflected in his pianos when he plays, and Chanel descends a staircase in her boutique with multiple panels of mirrors reflecting her luxurious movements. Mirrors are on nearly every wall in Chanel's house, a testament to her preoccupation with appearances. Mirrors are positioned behind characters, between them, and sometimes we see the central action in the film unfolding through a mirror. Characters stare at one another through clear, translucent, and semi-opaque windows.

Stravinsky and his son play chess with one another, each side of the board mirroring the other. An audience riots even as the sacrificial rites of an ancient pagan spring are enacted on a stage, which is another mirror of reality, with performers serving as a type of mirror to those who watch them. The composer (Stravinsky) steps behind the stage and sees the audience, his work met with their hooting and derisive insults. Stravinsky and his wife, Katya, mirror one another's discontent. Katya converses with Chanel, a mirror backgrounded, and reflects on the ways her marriage was once as perfect as the passion her husband has encountered again only through adultery.

Photographs represent people long gone, and the glass of their frames reflect the faces of those who study them. Mirrors in Chanel's bedroom are covered in mourning for her former lover; black drapes, which are uncovered by the curious Stravinsky who steals into rooms where he is not supposed to go. Chanel smears her hands across Stravinsky's spectacles and he wipes them clean. Chanel No. 5 becomes a reflection on femininity, just as the *Rite of Spring* becomes a reflection on a love affair which is only *presumed* to have happened between Igor and Coco. Our first view of Stravinsky is of him studying himself in a dressing room mirror, before performance.

From the opening credits, which appear to be kaleidoscoping mirrors, to the end credits, which present the same repeated unfolding of reflective patterns, to the colors black and white, which continually oppose and reflect one another in the color scheme of the film, *Coco Chanel and Igor Stravinsky* is a virtual orgy of mirrors, of reflections and pairings that defy sustainability or concretion. What about an essayist, bound to ponder mirrors with such a wretched affection that she must acknowledge staring into them, to reflect, and so reflecting find that she must look at herself every time she comes to a blank screen or sheet of paper, and fill it with words?

What about the mirror of the self, that endlessly excites and charms an artist to perform, to construct, to believe in communicating the self to others? There's no end to these lists of glass, of ways to see one's self in every facet, under every light, not to admire, but merely to see and study. Can we forgive the one who ponders his reflection because he sees flaws and is captivated by their enumeration? Is the self-conscious wallflower nearly as conceited as the vain extrovert, in thinking that everyone must see right clear to her soul? No one is that interesting all of the time; a thought that simultaneously consoles and punishes.

: :

My strenuous noting of each and every instance of mirroring and reflection in *Coco Chanel and Igor Stravinsky* shows how much I invested of my time and energy into what I'd hoped would be a serious, positive review of the film. In other ways, my ill-fated affair was also an investment in what turned out to be an illusion. We might say that I was taken in by "smoke and mirrors," or that the reality I inhabited was a just a reflection of my own consciousness, like Plato's cave allegory where the shadows on the wall are imperfect substitutes for what is real in the sunlight, in the open expression of day.

For me, that day dawned after a freakishly rainy summer, when I looked into the mirror of my own self and saw someone else reflected there. I began to realize that we had both deceived ourselves, with what we had wanted to see in each other upon first meeting. This is perhaps the most disconcerting moment in the film *Coco Chanel and Igor Stravinsky*: when both Igor and Coco wake up to the ways they had been misperceiving one another since the beginning. The transition into their final love scene begins with her working late at night. Chanel glances into her bedroom mirror and sees her reflection, while remembering their last conversation.

She asks him to come with her to Paris. He says he can't. She responds: "It's as if I don't exist for you. It's not enough anymore. I'm tired of it. You think a man is worth two women? You can't even compose without Catherine to correct it." Igor puts on his spectacles as she says, "I'm as powerful as you, Igor. And more successful." Hurt, Stravinsky retaliates: "You're not an artist, Coco. You're a shopkeeper." She says, "Get out," and we know the affair is over. For them, the wounds have everything to do with how they perceive themselves as artists, not with how they claim to feel about one another.

There is a boundary, no matter how much we claim to love someone and wish to please, between what serves the self and what serves two people equally, beyond measure. When Shakespeare writes in Sonnet 116, "Let me not to the marriage of true minds / Admit impediments," I think he pleads the way remain open between those who love each other truly. "Love is not love / Which alters when it alteration finds" seems to suggest that love survives entropy. If our love reworks itself in light of every flaw, it is not love that guides us, but something else entirely. Lukewarm affection, or its opposite, erotic desire, will never fulfill this definition.

All masks come free, and what was formerly perfect is effaced, and dull, not glimmering and beauteous as it was initially. We may wonder if we are turning away because we see something ugly about ourselves, a new sin in the portrait of Dorian Gray which we paint in secret, fearing exposure. Pleasure becomes the sickness we suffer by. Too much analysis and all love, real or imagined, disintegrates completely. One or two sentences later, someone says "get out" or "goodbye," and there is no question that forever is meant. Love becomes loathing in just a few permutations; a theme that plays itself into reverse, no less musical for being upside down.

: :

Months later, I'm listening to the *Rite of Spring*, in my thirty-ninth autumn, colored by heartbreak. I spend the day wondering what it is that people who are in love have that others only catch in fleeting glimpses. When I look back, there was a time in every love relationship I've known when it seemed as if we heard the same piece of music, each note as pure and pitched as a tuner might hear them, a matter of frequencies and adjusted tension. I believe that people who fall in love and stay in love have end philosophies that remain coherent, even after years of changes. Shared teleologies make for excellent marriages.

God or science? Fervent believers and their zealous opposites enjoy a grounding in love with their own kind, that free-range philosophers and anarchic thinkers merely skate around. Love is a passing fit for people disconnected from solid faiths. A fancy that glimmers in the light then breaks if it is set down too hard. The discordant notes of a pianist's slipping hand, the broken E-string on a violin overtaxed. Soon, the happiness that forms the chords for one ear becomes the contradiction in the ear of some other, and the whole composition dissolves. I acknowledge with some despondency that pleasure is a momentary perfection. What grace in seconds, before they are gone.

I might be a disillusioned romantic, if this means that I have parted ways with illusion itself. I've been scourged by my own self-deception. I'm wary of falling prey to my own idealism with someone else, who looks too familiar, seems too right. Even so, I maintain a belief in lifelong partnership, and I try to seek it out, to test it. A true romantic would not be moved by anything less than fire-swallowing, coal-walking proof of love. In the past, I've been the one doing most of the walking and burning. I've set myself on fire before with scant regard for equity. Let's blame it on passion, naïveté, too much hope.

Whether I'm reading Jacques Lacan, or studying the self-portraiture of Egon Schiele, I find myself making ridiculous, circular statements that stand as tautologies, like two mirrors facing one another reflecting into something approaching mathematical infinity. *Two narcissists walk into a bar mirror and one of them reflects.* It's the beginning of a bad philosophical joke with the punch line devolving into a repeating first line. *Two mirrors walk into a narcissist and both of them break.* I'm not afraid of the bad luck that's bound to result from breaking a sentence. It's not unlucky if you break an essay as long as you put all of the pieces back together again eventually.

Maybe I've only ever seen what I wanted to instead of what was actually there, and assumed meaning in complex correspondences. This kind of compulsiveness is a prerequisite for narcissists, and of all things to admit to, I'd hate for this to be true. I'd rather talk about mirrors, and a film about two egoists who are long dead, than suggest that I fell in love with a man in love with himself, because I was in love with myself too. Is this another circular obsession falling into delusion? What if I was the reason for his polyamory? That's the trouble with theorizing about mirrors: fear of seeing one's self too clearly.

AN INTERVIEW WITH COMPOSER IGOR STRAVINSKY

Igor Stravinsky's controversial ballet, *The Rite of Spring,* caused an uproar when it premiered in 1913 Paris, transforming listeners' musical expectations. In 2013, the 100th anniversary of the ballet's premiere, *Fugue State Magazine* met with Maestro Stravinsky to discuss his work *Poetics of Music: In the Form of Six Lessons,* first published by Harvard University Press in 1942.[18] Surprisingly, much of Stravinsky's poetics provides a critical heuristic for the personal essay, a matter that we explore here. Our guiding questions asked whether Maestro Stravinsky was thinking only about music when he first gave the lectures that would define his poetics, or whether readers can see him plumbing a deeper question about art in general. With great energy, Stravinsky begins by explaining his position as a theorist.

Stravinsky: I am a chair of poetics, which is the study of work to be done. The verb "poiein" from which the word is derived means nothing else but "to do" or "make." Ultimately, you will take from me whatever I may be capable of giving. And because my poetics are, in a sense, a series of confessions, most readers will take from them in the manner of their chosen art.[19]

FSM: So, it would not be unusual then for me to apply your poetics to the study of my chosen art, the personal essay? To *essay*— or, in Middle French "to attempt," from the Old French *essai,* "to put to proof, test the mettle of"—could also be, as you have said before when defining *explication*, "to describe something, to discover its genesis, to note the relationship of things to each other, to seek to throw light upon them."[20] Even from the beginning of your lectures you seem to be grounding your method in the realm of criticism, which is a territory of the essay. But it also seems quite personal to you—almost *essayistic*. How do we see you offering up an explanation of your own aesthetic in this work?

Stravinsky: To explain myself to you is also to explain myself to myself and to be obliged to clear up matters that are distorted or betrayed by the ignorance and malevolence that one always finds united by some mysterious bond in most of the judgments that are passed upon the arts.[21]

FSM: Could you discuss for a moment the difficulty artists encounter with conceptualizing a unified poetics when there are so many diverse artistic mediums? Recent years have found writers working within the broad category of nonfiction either deliberately aligning themselves with the Montaignean essay, and disregarding the more marketable memoir or narrative strains, or, defining themselves *against* the personal essay, which they see as a narcissistic, hyperintellectual enterprise. I sometimes wonder what holds all of nonfiction together, and what it is that prose poets, and lyrical, narrative, or personal essayists, as well as memoirists or academic writers have in common with one another.

Stravinsky: It seems that the unity we are seeking is forged without our knowing it and establishes itself within the limits which we impose on our work.[22]

FSM: There are a number of limits that appear to unify writers of nonfiction. When not arguing about matters of subgeneric classification, conversations turn to truth value—at least they did several years ago over James Frey's *A Million Little Pieces*, Lauren Slater's *Lying*, and the cat in Annie Dillard's *Pilgrim at Tinker Creek*. Or, there's the matter of attribution, raised by David

Shields in *Reality Hunger*. For a writer to quote another writer's work directly and not provide quotation marks raises questions about context and copyright. More recently, the argument was over John D'Agata's *The Lifespan of a Fact*. It seems that nonfiction is continually moving from one startling revelation to another, regarding what is acceptable, artful, and true.

Stravinsky: It was in 1912, in Berlin, when my *Firebird* and my *Petruschka* were played by the Russian Ballet. The Kaiser was there, even, and so I saw all the generals, and so on. And after us . . . they say . . . "too much noise." I want to say, "Where exactly?" You know, the scandals which were *à la mode* fifty years ago are not *à la mode* today.[23]

FSM: Or maybe, sometimes they are? Let us not forget Lillian Hellman's appropriated character in *Pentimento* who smuggled American passports to Jews living in Nazi Germany, hiding the documents in a fur hat. Hellman's Julia was based on the real-life experiences of antifascist activist Muriel Gardiner, whose memoirs were published in 1983. Hellman and Gardiner shared the same lawyer, which accounts for how Hellman encountered her material, but doesn't explain the ethical problem created by fabricating a character [Julia] in her memoir, and claiming to have assisted "Julia" with her work against the Nazis. In some ways we are still arguing over the same issues. Who can say what really happened, and to whom, and what's at stake beneath these expectations? To return to some of the ways a nonfiction writer might violate the "rules," beyond copyright issues and unattributed quotation, is it exploitative to put words in the mouths of others who cannot speak for themselves, even in playful, imagined dialogue? Or, regarding art in general: can there be ways that we push the envelope of truth value without violating it completely, by submitting more to the imagination than memory?

Stravinsky: Imagination is not only the mother of caprice but the servant and handmaiden of the creative will as well.[24] . . . What concerns us here is not imagination in itself, but rather creative imagination: the faculty that helps us to pass from the level of conception to the level of realization.[25] . . . The creator's function is to sift the elements he receives from her, for human activity must impose limits upon itself. The more art is controlled, limited, worked over, the more it is free.[26]

FSM: Let's come at this question from another direction, regarding limits and the imagination. "David Lazar in Conversation with Robert Burton, author of *Anatomy of Melancholy* (1621), *vox es, praeterea nihil*," which appeared in *Essay Daily* in September 2013, is an interview that never took place, given that both writers are separated by several centuries. Despite the wild, imaginative turn toward fantasy, Lazar is careful to actually quote Robert Burton, even as he creates the illusion of dialogue, which maintains a strong sense of order and unity in the piece. Additionally, the essay is kept brief, no doubt because a longer braiding of Lazar's prose and Burton's antiquated diction would be unsustainable. It's a sort of "found" interview, in the same way that poetry can be found . . . perhaps music too?

Stravinsky: I was guided by no system whatever in *Le Sacre du printemps*. Very little immediate tradition lies behind *Le Sacre du printemps*, and no theory. I had only my ear to help me. I heard, and I wrote what I heard. I am the vessel through which *Le Sacre* passed.[27]

FSM: I'm not sure if it's the same, although any writer might also imagine being the vessel through which words come. I mean the aspect of discovery that comes from arrangement. From careful editing and selection.

Stravinsky: All art presupposes a work of selection. Usually when I set to work my goal is not definite. If I were asked what I wanted at this stage of the creative process, I should be hard pressed to say. But I should always give an exact answer when asked what I did *not* want. To proceed by elimination—to know how to *discard*, as the gambler says, that is the great technique of selection. The principle of this method reveals the subconscious activity that makes us incline towards unity; for we instinctively prefer coherence and its quiet strength to the restless powers of dispersion—that is, we prefer the realm of order to the realm of dissimilarity.[28]

FSM: So Lazar's self-imposed "rule" to quote Burton verbatim provides stability, because there is at least one law in place that is not violated?

Stravinsky: A mode of composition that does not assign itself limits becomes pure fantasy.[29] . . . It is a fact of experience, and one that is only seemingly paradoxical, that we find freedom in a strict submission to the object. Let us take the best example: the fugue, a pure form in which the music means nothing outside itself. Doesn't the fugue imply the composer's submission to the rules? And is it not within those strictures that he finds the full flowering of his freedom as a creator? Strength, says Leonardo da Vinci, is born of constraint and dies in freedom.[30]

FSM: What I'm really wanting you to comment on is the framing of an essay as an interview, with someone long dead. Isn't this a *revolutionary* approach, given the way nonfiction writers have insisted that the prose be truthful stories about real people, who are still alive?

Stravinsky: Why burden the dictionary of the fine arts with this stertorous term, which designates in its most usual acceptation a state of turmoil and violence, when there are so many other words better adapted to designate originality? . . . [Suddenly emphatic.] To speak of revolution is to speak of a temporary chaos. Now art is the contrary of chaos. It never gives itself up to chaos without immediately finding its living works, its very existence, threatened. I approve of daring, I set no limits to it. But likewise there are no limits to the mischief wrought by arbitrary acts.[31]

FSM: Arbitrary acts . . . what would this mean for an essay? Are you saying that experimentation cannot emerge from an arbitrary model, such as a formal constraint in the manner of Oulipo? Not to say, of course, that all constraint is arbitrary. It's just a method, which, when not derived organically from a context, can become arbitrary, and in some cases, excessively abstract.

Stravinsky: The person who is loath to borrow these forms when he has need of them clearly betrays his weakness.[32] . . . [Grows quiet, but then holds up his hand to show he has more to say.] Gratuitous excess spoils every substance, every form that it touches. In its blundering it impairs the effectiveness of the most valuable discoveries and at the same time corrupts the taste of its devotees—which explains why their taste often plunges without transition from the wildest complications to the flattest banalities.[33]

FSM: Perhaps then, the best way any artist can argue on the behalf of his or her own aesthetic principles, is to create works that transform the criticism that attends them? Because criticism is at home in the essay, it seems that there are number of principles that writers often defend in their own work, or seek to overturn. As I've already suggested, truth value seems inherent to nonfiction, overall, given the amount of attention paid to it. When borrowing from other sources, attribution is expected, even indirectly; by this, homage is paid to the commonplace book and the conversations Montaigne had with the ancients. Memoirists recall what they can, albeit imperfectly, and must interrogate memory while demonstrating fairness to the memories of others. These are normative and formal constraints of genre.

Stravinsky: Well, in art as in everything else, one can build only upon a resisting foundation: whatever constantly gives way to pressure, constantly renders movement impossible. My freedom thus consists in my moving about within the narrow frame that I have assigned myself for each one of my undertakings.[34] Certainly though, we can make use of these forms without running the risk of becoming academic ourselves.[35] Since criticism is an art, it cannot itself escape our criticisms.[36] . . . In truth, we want it to be entirely free in its proper functioning which consists of judging existing works and not of maundering over the legitimacy of their origins or intentions.[37] It is my conviction that the public always shows itself more honest in its spontaneity than do those who officially set themselves up as judges of works of art.[38]

FSM: Are you saying that an audience might not be concerned with truth value, attribution, or the quality of one's memory? That critics may be the only ones asking these questions? Or that readers ultimately determine what succeeds as art? This seems to run counter with your experience, when your own *Rite of Spring* prompted brawls in the Théâtre des Champs-Élysées.

Stravinsky: [Momentarily flustered.] The storm broke. It was full of very noisy public. I get up, I said, "Go to Hell!"[39] They were very naïve and stupid people. It has nothing to do with art.[40]

FSM: I apologize for bringing up a difficult memory.

Stravinsky: All things considered, I prefer the forthright invective of the simple listener who has understood nothing to all the hollow praises that are as completely meaningless to those who proffer them as to those who receive them.[41] While music is constantly changing, the commentators who refuse to take note of these transformations do not themselves change. I am polemical not in my own defense, but in order to defend in words all music and its principles, just as I defend them in a different way with my compositions.[42]

FSM: Any artist can relate to what you say here. It is sometimes difficult for me to avoid the temptation to become polemical myself, since my own essays and those by others so often need defending against those who question the value of reflective writing about the self. Lately I've felt compelled to work more carefully within a strict frame, and I sometimes wonder if there is an element of masochism present when I subordinate my natural instinct for essaying and digressing to a set word count, or a structure that compels me toward unlikely outcomes.

Stravinsky: In a very general sense the principles of submission and insubordination characterize the attitude of the classicist and the romanticist before a work of art; a purely theoretic division, moreover, for we shall always find at the origin of invention an irrational element on which the spirit of submission has no hold and that escapes all constraint. That is what André Gide has so well expressed in saying that classical works are beautiful only by virtue of their subjugated romanticism. What is salient in this aphorism is the necessity for subjugation.[43]

FSM: An essayist then subjugates his or her writing to these ethical constraints: to tell the truth, to quote responsibly, to honor memory? Or do you mean formal kinds of constraints, in the same way a poet attempts the villanelle or sonnet, or a musician the fugue or a canon? How do you respond to constraint?

Stravinsky: "It is evident," writes Baudelaire, "that rhetorics and prosodies are not arbitrarily invented tyrannies, but a collection of rules demanded by the very organization of the spiritual being, and never have prosodies and rhetorics kept originality from fully manifesting itself. The contrary, that is to say, that they have aided the flowering of originality, would be infinitely more true."[44] [Strikes his chest with his palm.] As for myself, I experience a sort of terror when, at the moment of setting to work and finding myself before the infinitude of possibilities that present themselves, I have the feeling that everything is permissible to me. If everything is permissible to me, the best and worst; if nothing offers me any resistance, then any effort is inconceivable, and I cannot use anything as a basis, and consequently every undertaking becomes futile.[45]

FSM: The infinite blank page . . . perhaps the reason why more than one writer has assumed a model or a form . . . to give birth to creativity?

Stravinsky: What delivers me from the anguish into which an unrestricted freedom plunges me is the fact that I am always able to turn immediately to the concrete things that are here in question. I have no use for a theoretic freedom. Let me have something finite, definite—matter that can lend itself to my operation only insofar as it is commensurate with my possibilities. And such matter presents itself to me together with its limitations. I must in turn impose mine upon it. So here we are, whether we like it or not, in the realm of necessity. And yet which of us has ever heard talk of art as other than a realm of freedom? This sort of heresy is uniformly widespread because it is imagined that art is outside the bounds of ordinary activity.[46]

FSM: I like how you see this process as one of give-and-take, instead of purely prescriptive and reductive. Maestro Stravinsky, you've written that "style is the particular way a composer organizes his conceptions and speaks the language of his craft."[47] If a writer or a composer continually works within a model in order to discover previously unknown elements of his or her craft, can this method become a kind of entrapment? And how does this kind of formal play advance the tradition itself, given that the writer or composer works within and with a structure instead of against it?

Stravinsky: The artist imposes a culture upon himself and ends by imposing it on others. That is how tradition becomes established.[48] Far from implying the repetition of what has been, tradition presupposes the reality of what endures. It appears as an heirloom, a heritage that one receives on condition of making it bear fruit before passing it on to one's descendants. . . . Tradition thus assures the continuity of creation.[49] . . . What is important for the lucid ordering of the work—for its crystallization—is that all the Dionysian elements which set the imagination of the artist in motion and make the life-sap rise must be properly subjugated before they intoxicate us, and must finally be made to submit to the law: Apollo demands it.[50] . . . I shall go even further: my freedom will be so much the greater and more meaningful the more narrowly I limit my field of action and the more I surround myself with obstacles. Whatever diminishes constraint, diminishes strength. The more constraints one imposes, the more one frees one's self of the chains that shackle the spirit.[51]

FSM: Do you then see inspiration as merely finding a shape, or imposing a structure? Are there no random provocations in composition?

Stravinsky: I simply maintain that inspiration is in no way a pre-scribed condition of the creative act, but rather a manifestation that is chronologically secondary.[52] . . . All creation presupposes at its origin a sort of appetite that is brought on by the foretaste of discovery. This foretaste of the creative act accompanies the intuitive grasp of an unknown entity already possessed but not yet intelligible, an entity that will not take definite shape except by the action of a constantly vigilant technique.[53] . . . The very act of putting my work on paper, of, as we say, kneading the dough, is for me inseparable from the pleasure of creation. So far as I am concerned, I cannot separate the spiritual effort from the psycho-logical and physical effort; they confront me on the same level and do not present a hierarchy.[54]

FSM: Essayists would argue the same—that much of the writing is about discovery that comes through practice, the act of writing. Still, I am sometimes provoked or inspired by something that comes to me outside of the writing act. A line perhaps. Or an idea for an essay. There's something like chance in these moments.

Stravinsky: This gift of chance must not be confused with that ca-priciousness of imagination that is commonly called fancy. Fancy implies a predetermined will to abandon one's self to caprice. The aforementioned assistance of the unexpected is something quite different.[55] [Begins to clean his spectacles, but deep in thought and already moving in another direction.] I am none the less convinced that by ceaselessly varying the search one ends up only in futile curiosity. That is why I find it pointless and dangerous to over-refine techniques of discovery. A curiosity that is attracted by everything betrays a desire for quiescence in multiplicity. Now this desire can never find true nourishment in endless variety. By developing it we acquire only a false hunger, a false thirst: they are false, in fact, because nothing can slake them.[56]

FSM: I see that you take everything, even apparent random inspira-tion, quite seriously. But are you truly so rigid with regard to the source for inspiration? Must we always be at our desks or pianos when a good idea comes to us? Surely there is some flexibility here.

Stravinsky: [Sighing, with a slow nod.] "In everything that yields gracefully," G. K. Chesterton says somewhere, "there must be resistance." Bows are beautiful when they bend only because they seek to remain rigid. Rigidity that slightly yields, like Justice swayed by Pity, is all the beauty of earth. Everything seeks to grow straight, and happily, nothing succeeds in so growing. Try to grow straight and life will bend you.[57]

FSM: Many of your metaphors emphasize an organic structure; something that arises from the moment in which one finds herself, or, from an appreciative grace. Could you say a bit more about this?

Stravinsky: All music being nothing but a succession of impulses and repose, it is easy to see that the drawing together and separation of poles of attraction in a way determine the respiration of music.[58] . . . The faculty of creating is never given to us all by itself. It always goes hand in hand with the gift of observation.[59]

FSM: The personal essay certainly has this quality of observation. And I amend my earlier remarks regarding the "randomness" of what inspires us. Really, we more often are walking, or driving, perhaps reading when an idea occurs to us. We are more often engaged in some indirect technique of our own composing process when inspiration comes. Say a bit more about observation?

Stravinsky: The true creator may be recognized by his ability always to find about him, in the commonest and humblest thing, items worthy of note.[60] . . . He does not have to put forth in search of discoveries: they are always within his reach. He will have only to cast a glance about him. Familiar things, things that are everywhere, attract his attention. The least accident holds his interest and guides his operations[61] . . . on occasion, he may draw profit from something unforeseen that a momentary lapse reveals to him.[62]

FSM: Patrick Madden's *Quotidiana* comes to mind. Madden's work typically circles and plumbs the simplest of subjects with enormous depth. He has always placed faith in discovery and surprise in his essays. But do you believe so much of an artist's work to be accidental? Why would we not try then to manufacture "accidents" in our lives just in order to make art from them? Sounds messy.

Stravinsky: One does not contrive an accident: one observes it to draw inspiration therefrom. An accident is perhaps the only thing that really inspires us. A composer improvises aimlessly the way an animal grubs about. Both of them go grubbing about because they yield to a compulsion to seek things out.[63]

FSM: It sounds as easy as breathing when you describe it. Before, when you spoke about *music* as respiration, it was easy to see that the drawing together and separation of poles of attraction in a way determine the respiration of the essaying aesthetic. Our slippages are the breath of essay, of attempting to know and describe one's changing self. If our experience separates from fact, becomes diverted by the imagination, then an uncomfortable interval is created between what we know and what we don't know about ourselves, that the reader can see and make use of.

Stravinsky: Oscar Wilde said that every author always paints his own portrait: what I observe in others must likewise be observable in me.[64]

FSM: Or, "We see things not as they are, but as we are ourselves," according to essayist H. M. Tomlinson? Perhaps, when writing our lives, many of us paint our own portraits through our characterizations of other people, as extensions of our own internal judgments and processes. Contradictions of character were not problematic to Montaigne, who embraced it in himself through his skepticism, his apologies for his bad memory, his overall unwillingness to commit to one perspective or philosophical point of view regarding personal experience. When he writes, "We are, I know not how, double within ourselves,"[65] he claims a verisimilitude of selfhood that is derived from being perennially split between two ways of being. How then can we rely on him to be accurate, without accepting the dissonance of his relation to himself?

Stravinsky: Ever since it appeared in our vocabulary, the word dissonance has carried with it a certain odor of sinfulness. . . . Dissonance is an element of transition, a complex or interval of tones which is not complete in itself and which must be resolved to the ear's satisfaction into a perfect consonance. But just as the eye completes the lines of a drawing which the painter has knowingly left incomplete, just so the ear may be called upon to complete a chord and cooperate in its resolution, which has not actually been realized in the work.[66]

FSM: So dissonance is an encouragement and a pleasure to the pattern-making mind. Like the *frisson* in a horror film that Philip Lopate describes in his introduction to *The Art of the Personal Essay*—the monster seeing itself in a mirror: The moment when we realize we are ourselves the monster.[67] Or the temptation to look under the sheet covering the corpse, as Stephen King writes in *Danse Macabre*. In another place he presages Lopate: "We have met the monster, and, as Peter Straub points out in *Ghost Story*, he is us."[68] Over and over again we confront the fear of knowing ourselves. Even that moment in *The Empire Strikes Back*, when Luke confronts Darth Vader on Dagobah and sees his own face beneath the mask. There are limitless examples of what I mean here.

Stravinsky: [Shaking his head slightly.] Dissonance, in this instance, plays the part of an allusion.[69] . . . For over a century music has provided repeated examples of a style in which dissonance has emancipated itself. It is no longer tied down to its former function. Having become an entity in itself, it frequently happens that dissonance neither prepares nor anticipates anything. Dissonance is thus no more an agent of disorder than consonance is a guarantee of security.[70]

FSM: By this, you mean that dissonance is written into our natures as human beings? As a transitional experience between falling out of order and of coming back into it?

Stravinsky: Individual caprice and intellectual anarchy, which tend to control the world in which we live, isolate the artist from his fellow artists and condemn him to appear as a monster in the eyes of the public; a monster of originality, inventor of his own language, of his own vocabulary, and of the apparatus of his art.[71] So he comes to the point of speaking an idiom without relation to the world that listens to him. His art becomes truly unique, in the sense that it is incommunicable and shut off on every side.[72] . . . Times have changed since the day when Bach, Handel, and Vivaldi quite evidently spoke the same language which their disciples repeated after them, each one unwittingly transforming this language according to his own personality.[73]

FSM: Given what you say here, and although you argue that dissonance is not an agent of disorder, how does everything hang together in a composition? Where is the center?

Stravinsky: Composing, for me, is putting into an order a certain number of these sounds according to certain interval-relationships. This activity leads to a search for the center upon which the series of sounds involved in my undertaking should converge. Thus, if a center is given, I shall have to find a combination that converges upon it. If, on the other hand, an as yet unoriented combination has been found, I shall have to determine the center towards which it should lead. The discovery of this center suggests to me the solution of my problem. It is thus that I satisfy my very marked taste for such a kind of musical typography.[74]

FSM: In which dissonance exists, along with consonance, without upsetting the structure. What kinds of decisions do you make when composing?

Stravinsky: In my brain, there are two things—interval and rhythm, which are the main elements of the music.[75] I still compose at the piano. You know why? When I compose myself, I have only to have the vibrations, the vibrations must be *pianissimo*, and then I hear every parcel (if I can say this way) of the sound.[76] I always like to compose music more than the music itself.[77]

FSM: Funny. I could say the same about writing, except that I feel I never have enough time available to me.

Stravinsky: [Shrugging.] I have no time. There are people who have time, people who have money.[78] [Holds out his outstretched hands.] The past slips from our grasp. It leaves us only scattered things.[79]

FSM: To shift the conversation some, the philosopher Gottfried Leibniz, in a Letter to Christian Goldbach, dated April 17, 1712, wrote that "music is a hidden arithmetic exercise of the soul, which doesn't know that it is counting." You explain in your *Poetics* that you intend to "study the phenomenon of music as a form of speculation in terms of sound and time." The derivation is, as you say, "the dialectics of the creative process" involving the "principle of contrast and similarity."

Stravinsky: Music presupposes before all else a certain organization in time, a chrononomy. . . . Thus we see that meter, since it offers in itself only elements of symmetry and is inevitably made up of even quantities, is necessarily utilized by rhythm, whose function it is to establish order in the movement by dividing up the quantities furnished in the measure.[80]

FSM: It's tempting to imagine how this could be done with the essay, by substituting "intimacy and syntax" for "sound and time." Essaying is a syntactical art, as music is a chronologic art. The measure of a sentence is syntactically the result of a symmetric relation between reflection and meaning, a way of ordering the relationships we maintain with others, and especially, with the self. Whether our prose advances thought forward, or lyrically circles a moment in the past, we function within the syntax of our writing, which establishes order in the movement by dividing up the quantities furnished in our personal experiences and philosophies. Virginia Tufte, in opening her book *Artful Sentences: Syntax as Style,* writes, "It is syntax that gives words the power to relate to each other in a sequence, to create rhythms and emphasis, to carry meaning—of whatever kind—as well as glow individually in just the right place."[81]

Stravinsky: Everyone knows that time passes at a rate which varies according to the inner dispositions of the subject and to the events that come to affect his consciousness. Expectation, boredom, anguish, pleasure and pain, contemplation—all of these thus come to appear as different categories in the midst of which our life unfolds, and each of these determines a special psychological process, a particular tempo. These variations in psychological time are perceptible only as they are related to the primary sensation—whether conscious or unconscious—of real time, ontological time.[82]

FSM: And thus meaning and reflection serve as limiters on syntax because of the way they embed human experience in the fabric of time.

Stravinsky: Music that is based on ontological time is generally dominated by the principle of similarity. The music that adheres to psychological time likes to proceed by contrast. To these two principles which dominate the creative process correspond the fundamental concepts of variety and unity. All the arts have recourse to this principle.[83]

FSM: I'm not sure that I follow. But then, I think of essays with numbered sections, which seem to launch an appeal for order at the same time texture and contrast is created within the work. It is a kind of "countable" prose.

Stravinsky: Contrast produces an immediate effect. Similarity satisfies us only in the long run. Contrast is an element of variety, but it divides our attention. Similarity is born of a striving for unity.[84]

FSM: In essays that are built on prose poem fragments, there is a way that each separate element, or each lyrical segment, speaks to the entire work. But then there is a reason for the lines' incremental separateness. As much we prefer unity, is there not a legitimate desire for variety, and spontaneity in a work?

Stravinsky: [Responding carefully, and slowly, with some tiredness.] The need to seek variety is perfectly legitimate, but we should not forget that the One precedes the Many. Moreover, the coexistence of both is constantly necessary, and all the problems of art, like all possible problems for that matter, including the problem of knowledge and of Being, revolve ineluctably about this question, with Parmenides on one side denying the possibility of the Many, and Heraclitus on the other denying the existence of the One. Mere common sense, as well as supreme wisdom, invite us to affirm both the one and the other.[85]

FSM: A good note to end on. Thank you so much, Maestro Stravinsky, for sharing your thoughts with us, and for considering the ways that your work can be helpful to those of us who compose with words. Any parting thoughts?

Stravinsky: [Smiling generously.] The true hierarchy of phenomena, as well as the true hierarchy of relationships, takes on substance and form on a plane entirely apart from that of conventional classifications.[86] A thousand obstacles separate us from the ancestral riches which yield to us only aspects of their dead reality. And even then we grasp them by intuition rather than by conscious knowing.[87] [Throws his hands up and laughs.]

ECHO'S FUGUE

Echo played chess with her lover deep into the night, drinking and smoking the occasional cigarette. She won only a bit more than half the time, but admired his fearless opening moves and his willingness to engage his queen right away. Echo was always the more defensive player, and had been all her life. Sometimes this was an asset. Most of the time it just made the game too long. Normally she didn't care about winning games, but chess was different. Perhaps her lover felt the same way, which is why he often suggested they make up their own rules. They theorized a hybrid: part Battleship, Stratego, and Chess.

"Blind Battle-Chess" required that they place a large blind in the middle of the board, then strategically place their pieces anywhere they liked. After they were content with their arrangements, they would remove the blind. They would roll the dice to see who went first, and then play out their battlements. Forever ago, when they were still in love, Echo recorded their positions in her notebook. She rolled an eleven, which meant she would go first, and he rolled a seven. It was late, so they put the pieces away, and went to bed. Many months passed, during which time they broke up, and Echo stopped carrying the notebook.

One night her former lover sent her a message, saying that he was in a polyamorous relationship, and would Echo like to come see him? They had been apart for eight months, and though she was still angry at him, she wanted to confirm what she already knew. He had begun dating a girl in her twenties, and six months into their relationship, he was inviting Echo over to his house for dinner. Evidence of the nymph wasn't hard to find; her flats in the living room said everything. She was coming back, this was going to be her home in three weeks. Echo had better not get comfortable.

Echo didn't know if he told the nymph the truth about Echo being there, but he said he did. Echo pulled out her notebook and set up the pieces as their last game had been. It ended in a draw. Echo learned that his new girlfriend wanted to have his baby, but he would have to reverse his vasectomy. He smiled uncomfortably when Echo suggested that the nymph was idealizing him. The next morning, he told Echo that the nymph liked older men, citing a scandalous teacher-affair in high school. Unfazed, Echo suggested psychology was complicating everything. He stared out the window as they drove back from the riverside.

: :

When they had broken up eight months before, he joined a social network that he had avoided the whole year they were together. He bought a computer, his wife moved out, his divorce was finalized, and he was ready to date multiple people simultaneously. This was a recipe for online volatility, and Echo was prepared to witness what she could see from afar, outside of the affair. Echo knew that she didn't want to be communicating with him or any member of his family or friends. Echo knew that she was volatile too, and overly preoccupied with discovering the truth behind things rather than take someone's word for it.

Sometimes Echo would grow curious, log in and search for his profile. She would try to figure out his dating behavior based on his online persona. Was he seeing the polyamorous BDSM sexual "edutainer" he had befriended the night they separated for good? Or this woman—the one he was talking so much about the last few times they were together? (She's ten years older than Echo.) Or maybe someone else entirely? Until one day, when Echo clicked on one girl's profile and saw she had posted a photo of herself with Echo's ex-lover and one of his children. Searching her name online told Echo a traumatic psycho-sexual history.

The nymph had been a minor, around the same time Echo's ex-lover had finished having children with his wife. She and her teacher were caught "engaging in sexual acts." The teacher's communications with her through email were "very sexual and controlling in nature," or so says the court report. (Echo wondered why the court report was posted publicly for anyone to see.) The teacher had proposed to the nymph, on the condition that she graduate and go on to college and give him enough time to divorce his wife. Ten years later, he is a registered sex offender in his sixties. Echo wonders if his wife stayed with him.

: :

A few months later, going through notebooks, Echo found their old chess game. She loaded it into an online program, and the computer beat her in just a few moves. Echo decided to see what would happen if a computer played both sides of the board. After placing the pieces in their appropriate places, Echo asked the computer to recommend a move. She did this also for the other side, after making the suggested move and requesting another recommendation. The results showed her that purely logical moves resulted in unrelenting casualties on both sides. Echo wondered if there were other possibilities, unexpected outcomes that only emerged with human players.

It took the computer forty moves to determine that check would be a repeating outcome. His white rook would indefinitely hold Echo's black king in thrall, endlessly vacillating between two islanded squares. His rook was the more mobile piece, and the openness of his particular arrangement—compared to Echo's closed walls that only blocked her in—worked to an undeniable advantage. It was a zero-sum game, tit-for-tat, where neither of them would win as long as both refused to resign. In so many ways, their relationship ended on those same terms, with her resistance forming walls that Echo considered unassailable. Every relationship with a polyamorist is tautologically polyamorous.

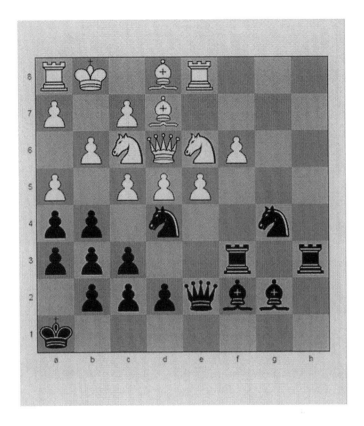

It did not matter if Echo had known that he was polyamorous from the outset, she would have attempted the relationship. Echo would have fallen in love, realized she needed more than he could give her. Echo would have failed to have been all he wanted. If she had known from the beginning, she might be less angry now, but she would not have experienced the thrill of asking the question: must I love the same person now and forever? Her experiences had left her with a line of disappointments stretching back to her childhood. Despite the self-pity she indulged, she began to see the ways she punished herself.

Bach was gone, and had been for years. Echo attended music festivals each summer, where she lost herself in live music. She stopped caring so deeply about the past. Her weakness had always been silence, and waiting for someone to shout into it. She wanted her undoing. Her attempts at self-preservation often resembled loneliness. The games play out in her head, and Echo sometimes saw the process as a long sapping that left her wondrous. What did she expect? What did Echo enjoy? Fleeing, chasing, *flight*. Perhaps how the playing broke her into ruins. Perhaps the ways she felt left with only two choices. To play, then play, again.

ENDGAME

On Some Versions of Venery

I'm not sure when I first discovered that the theoretical game known as "Battle of the Sexes" was also known as "Bach or Stravinsky" (BoS). It was well after I had begun to study fugues, and an imaginary Bach had been visiting me for months. Perhaps I had also begun to listen to Stravinsky, but my guess is that my interest in him grew after my discovery of the BoS motif in Martin J. Osborne and Ariel Rubinstein's *A Course in Game Theory*.

Labeled "EXAMPLE 15.3 (*Bach or Stravinsky? (BoS)*)," this classic textbook problem is deceptively simple: "Two people wish to go out together to a concert of music by either Bach or Stravinsky. Their main concern is to go out together, but one person prefers Bach and the other person prefers Stravinsky." It is the situation of date night happening all over the world; two people have different ideas about what they enjoy when alone, but they want to be together. The authors continue, explaining that "the game has two Nash equilibria: (*Bach, Bach*) and (*Stravinsky, Stravinsky*). That is, there are two steady states: one in which both players always choose *Bach* and one in which they always choose *Stravinsky*.88 It helps to understand that a steady state is when each player knows what to expect from the other and acts rationally; in other words, they choose the outcome with the greatest payoff. For the average person not knowing anything about game theory, the idea of steady states seems like overthinking. If I knew what my partner was going to do, even without discussing beforehand, we would be sharing a stability that made sense; in my thinking, we would maximize the peace that a steady, predictable life brings. But that is the kind of fool I am and always have been.

Game theory had become a fascination during the time I was most obsessed with finding hidden meanings in song lyrics, and I was angry for loving someone who did not love me back. I nervously thumbed through John Maynard Smith's *Did Darwin Get It Right: Essays on Games, Sex, and Evolution,* looking for an answer I didn't find the first time when I'd studied it in a philosophy class twenty years before. My instincts were aligned with what I felt to be true: love was indeed a kind of game, and any theory about it would have to take into account every aspect of the analogy.

I made a playlist called "Game Theory" with songs like "The Gambler," "One Night in Bangkok," "Poker Face," and Peter Jöback's collaborative cover (with Sia) of Chris Isaak's "Wicked Game." (I still favor the original). "Your Cheatin' Heart" was a staple of the theme as well as Little River Band's "Lonesome Loser." I found four dozen or so songs that varied between personal favorites like R.E.M.'s "Endgame" and songs I'd only recently begun to try to decipher, such as "Video Games" by Lana Del Ray. "Love Is a Losing Game" croons Amy Winehouse just before the list shuffles to Lily Allen's "Not Fair." Lenny Kravitz's "Straight Cold Player" balances funk against ABBA's pristine harmonies in "The Winner Takes It All." Boy George's "The Crying Game," which will always dredge up a memory of Forest Whitaker's tragic love in the Irish-British film by the same name. Beck's "Loser," which captures the summer after my second year in college. I was, at the time, on the verge of what I considered fantastic breakthroughs of consciousness, as I had been experimenting with LSD and smoking herb every chance I found.

Lest I stray too far, my early internet searches on the BoS coordination game turned up more results for Battle of the Sexes than for Bach or Stravinsky. In the original version of the game a man and a woman plan to spend their evening together at either a prize fight or the ballet, and "following the usual cultural stereotype, the man much prefers the fight and the woman the ballet." These gendered elements of the game detailed in the 1957 book *Games and Deci-*

sions: Introduction and Critical Survey by R. Duncan Luce and Howard Raiffa contribute to the problem: "to both it is more important that they go out together than that each see the preferred entertainment."[89]

The authors consider several challenges facing the couple. One involves preplay discussion wherein "it is advantageous in such a situation to disclose one's strategy first and have a reputation for inflexibility."[90] If, for instance, the man already has tickets to the fight and is determined to go, the woman may "submit to his will." Or, and I love the wording here: "to some spirited females, such an offhand dictatorial procedure is presented with sufficient ferocity to alter drastically the utilities involved in the payoff matrix," which is another way of saying that he'll be taking someone else to the fight, and she'll be going to the ballet.

Another complication is the possibility of their not talking beforehand about their plans or forgetting what they decided, which puts both in the position of deciding simultaneously and independently. This is more often the version of the game people encounter first when studying Battle of the Sexes, though sometimes the prize fight is changed to a football game and the ballet becomes the opera. The main point though is that each player is responding to the strategies of the other, and both want to be together, regardless of where they end up.

In the spirit of updating the game's description, Martin J. Osborne and Ariel Rubinstein changed the evening's entertainment to that of a musical concert in their 1994 text, *A Course in Game Theory*. Two people want to spend the evening together, but one prefers the music of Bach and the other, Stravinsky.

To be certain of the game's original nomenclature, I emailed both authors, and received a response from Dr. Osborne who confirmed that they not only originated the name change but also seemed to be the only ones who preferred it, given the male-dominated nature of their profession. "We do not like the stereotypes embedded in this interpretation, and when writing our book, *A Course in Game Theory*, sought a neutral name. I also strongly reject the notion underlying the 'Battle of the Sexes' interpretation that men and women have fundamentally different preferences and are thus necessarily involved in a 'battle.'" Better even, the mystery behind Osborne and Rubenstein's choice of composers was revealed: "We looked for options for entertainment about which people could disagree, and wanted to preserve the acronym for the game, BoS. I'm not sure what led us specifically to 'Bach or Stravinsky?' I guess we looked for composers with shortish names starting with B and S."[91]

Despite this seemingly arbitrary decision, I'm delighted that it didn't end up Brahms or Shostakovich. It could also have been Beethoven or Schumann, even Bartók or Strauss. But Bach and Stravinsky are distinct from one another in so many ways none of the others can be. Furthermore, I find that removing the gender stereotyping opens the game more widely to my understanding, as a scenario anyone could find other equivalent metaphors for, including preferences for sexual behavior in a relationship. What if, for instance, both parties have not discussed in advance of their sexual involvement whether they are engaging in lovemaking or fucking? Clearly, both parties would benefit pleasurably in the moment by having sex, but only one individual in half of the possible payoffs would be satisfied by not only enjoying carnal delights, but also being fulfilled emotionally. Someone would be deceived in either case, though I'm not yet ready to consider to what extent I can even articulate it. Whenever we go to bed with other people for the first time, we hope to find some kind of reliable equilibrium on which we both agree.

Or, we could further challenge the matrix by saying that in one scenario, Player 1 and Player 2 have been dating for six months, and that Player 1 is monoamorous and that Player 2 is polyamorous. In either case, they each prefer a kind of relationship that the other doesn't, and yet they love one another and want to stay together as long as possible.

Let's up the ante and say that there is limited preplay communication other than a vague understanding of preferences. We might see a payoff wherein Player 2 stays faithful to Player 1, thereby compromising a preference for multiple partners, but at least maintaining the relationship with Player 1. We will also see a payoff where Player 1 and Player 2 both decide to take on other lovers, and though Player 1 is uncomfortable with the choice, the relationship remains intact with Player 2, who is happily exploring relationships with other people.

Nobody wins in a scenario where Poly-Player 2 (predictably) cheats on Mono-Player 1 who (predictably) remains faithful, or one in which Mono-Player 1 (quite unexpectedly!) is seduced and Poly-Player 2 turns down a spontaneous orgy because Player 1 isn't present to approve, watch, or participate. This last payoff will spark resentment, accusations of hypocritical behavior, and ultimately lead to separation. On the contrary, one in which both Players have cooperated in choosing the same terms for their relationship suggests that at least one person is capable of self-sacrifice.

We can see the payoffs in Figure 3, where both strategies for each player are played out, in a way that should reveal how little I understand about game theory. Or, perhaps I've chosen the wrong game completely?

Player 2

		Infidelity	Fidelity
	Infidelity	1, 2	0, 0
Player 1	Fidelity	0, 0	2, 1

TO CHEAT OR NOT TO CHEAT?

A few years ago my boyfriend at the time decided that he was polyamorous and perhaps had always been. I looked for answers that could help me decide what I should do, and how I should feel. I found *More Than Two: Franklin Veaux's Polyamory Site,* and there, a page titled "A Dialog between a Polyamorous and a Monogamous Person." It wasn't until I arrived at the ultimate description of what a relationship between the two might be, that I froze with recognition of a paradox: "Ultimately, a mono/poly relationship is a polyamorous relationship. No matter what structures you impose on it, it's still, by its nature, a polyamorous relationship." If an attempt to translate this into a payoff table looks ridiculous, it is no less confusing than the last six months of our relationship.

Perhaps instead of BoS, we should consult the matrix of the Prisoner's Dilemma, another classic game theory model. In the original, two individuals suspected of a crime are offered sweeter deals for betraying the other, even though, should they both choose to keep silent, they would benefit equally. In Figure 4, my version is played out with a similar scenario as the BoS game above, though their choices in my version of the Prisoner's Dilemma translates into reverse payoffs of the classic scenario. But let's give it a go, shall we?

Player 2

		Poly	*Mono*
	Poly	3, 3	5, 0
Player 1	*Mono*	0, 5	1, 1

POLY OR MONO?

This may capture the problem better than my last attempt.

If both Player 1 and Player 2 behave polyamorously, that is—they both engage in intimate relationships with multiple partners—both reap a shared and equal benefit through cooperation which may also exponentially increase their risks for venereal disease (but never mind about *that*). Or, if both decide to remain monogamously paired, they look forward to a "domestic gulag"[92] of diminishing returns with regard to their libidos. But, if one or the other attempt to remain monogamous while the other partner chooses polyamory, the mono partner receives a large "L" planted over the forehead, just so, as in Figure 5:

UNIVERSAL SIGN FOR LOSER, OR THE "SUCKER'S PAYOFF"

But perhaps I am behind the times.

It isn't that I don't appreciate the sense of freedom that comes with polyamorous relationships. It's just that I'm doubtful that when payoffs are low (the kids are sick, the debts are piling up, or your partner is too tired for sex and would rather simply vent frustrations) that anyone would choose a relationship at all. The payoffs of being alone or of behaving selfishly appear to be much higher than those of cooperation. And though I can't find a reasonable game model to represent my exact situation, I search for a way to puzzle out a problem of long-lasting significance.

What would a game look like if players chose to behave as either Echo or Narcissus? In the case where two individuals both care too much about themselves, or conversely, neither care much for themselves, there can be no payoff. Figure 6 shows two individuals in both cases with an undesirable payoff of 0, 0. But in the cases where Player 1 or Player 2 acts only out of self-interest, the reward is clear, with no discernable limit to how far the game can be taken, so long as someone else is willing to be exploited:

Player 2

		Narcissus	Echo
	Narcissus	0, 0	+1, −1
Player 1			
	Echo	−1, +1	0, 0

NARCISSUS OR ECHO?

These charming diagrams of mine explain nothing, aside from illuminating some kind of bitterness in me that has long existed. I feel that I am both Narcissus and Echo, and have been throughout my life. I can see the conflict internal to me: to remain alone, assuming responsibility for my own happiness and spurning outside interests because they can hurt me, or they are not engaging or desirable enough. And in those cases where *I am* attracted, I see only those qualities in my own self that are familiar: the need to be in control, made easier by being alone, and the lack of interest in externalizing desire. There is only the reflection, the amusement of the glinting water, and in someone else, the endless refractions of light. If I love you, it is because you love yourself too much. If you do not notice me, I will want you more.

Hamilton Leithauser + Rostam's 2016 song, "A 1000 Times," in direct lyrical quotation is as much a poem about love and loss as it is a song of irresistible appeal; in part because of the lyrics, in part for the vocals and piano, in part because we all know this feeling. Even when I omit the repetition that might have been a *ritornello* or *rondo* in the age of Bach, we hear his driving pain multiplied many times over. Is there much difference between a virtuoso like Glenn Gould taking the repeat and this driving chorus that painfully enumerates obsession? "I had a dream that you were mine / I've had that dream a thousand times."[93]

The remarkable thing is how obsessive it all becomes, the reiteration of desire that is mistaken for love. I will repeat my song like an unwelcome morning bird. I will wear myself out until I am an echo of the originating desire. With so much out of the way, I will repeat the cycle with someone else, creating stable equilibria, where at least there is some payoff in trying.

: :

The book that triggered my polyamorous ex to redefine our relationship was *Sex at Dawn: How We Mate, Why We Stray, and What It Means for Modern Relationships* by psychologist Christopher Ryan and his wife, psychiatrist Cacilda Jethá. *Sex at Dawn* was a 2010 *New York Times* bestseller, and several academics responded to it with ample criticism and others with limited praise. The book argues that monogamy is not natural to human beings and that women are inherently promiscuous, despite predominant cultural beliefs to the contrary. In one place Ryan and Jethá explicitly state that "a great deal of research from primatology, anthropology, anatomy, and psychology points to the same fundamental conclusion: human beings and our hominid ancestors have spent almost all of the past few million years or so in small, intimate bands in which most adults had several sexual relationships at any given time."[94] In other places they are less eloquent, when criticizing the trade-offs a woman accepts in marriage: "Darwin says your mother's a whore. Simple as that."[95]

Perhaps it's the reductionism that I react to, even as much as I crave it as a simple way through every complex system. Arguments that take as base precepts sociobiological reasons for human beings' behavior always seem too narrow. That could be because so many thinkers neglect the way culture changes the environment in which we evolve, well past the point it was initially. For instance—readily available birth control and a declining utility for marriage has changed the way heterosexual men and women consider their commitments to one another. Co-parenting is possible between divorced couples in a way hitherto inconceivable twenty years ago.

Openness toward a spectrum of gender and sexual preferences have likewise released a flood of exploration. I would be willing to believe that human beings, like every other animal, are primarily driven to reproduce if I didn't know so many people now for whom sex is a *recreation* with procreation as an undesirable outcome. I'm also assuming that people weren't that different a thousand years ago, or even two thousand years ago, with regard to balancing sexual desire with the sometimes necessary transactions of culture. Of course evolution favored those generations of human beings who successfully reproduced and didn't content themselves with casting their seed onto the ground. But it's far too complicated a story for one paragraph, or even for an entire essay, book-length or otherwise.

Soon after my lover began to study *Sex at Dawn* and use it as a justification for what he considered an ideal relationship, I read it too and became frustrated and angry. Some lines stood out to me as deliberately provocative, but limited in terms of support. I felt Ryan and Jethá's attacks against the so-called "standard narrative" equated to cherry-picking. I also believed that their book's success was a response to a social trend that had already been moving away from monogamy for decades, so any argument they put up as coming from a seemingly scientific source would be well received, without question. I still think much of this to be the case. But when they write that "the essence of sexuality for most women seems to include the freedom to change as life changes around them,"[96] something shifts in me, for this has been my experience. There is no question that the book promotes polyamory and promiscuity, especially with regard to women. They quote *The Ethical Slut* by Dossie Easton and Catherine Lizt, who write:

> It is cruel and insensitive to interpret an affair as a symptom of sick-
> ness in the relationship, as it leaves the "cheated-on" partner—who
> may already be feeling insecure—to wonder what is wrong with
> him. . . . Many people have sex outside their primary relationships
> for reasons that have nothing to do with any inadequacy in their
> partner or in the relationship.[97]

Having felt insecure and "cheated-on" before, I try to remember what my response was then, which is something I've tried to forget ever since. I recall how, when my husband confessed a moment of infidelity, I suggested to him that we move to an open marriage or else plan to divorce. Initially he seemed to favor the first suggestion, but then decided it was impossible. By that time I had already begun to feel extramarital attraction for someone else, and this change in me signaled the end for our marriage. I moved from seeing myself as a victim to someone prepared to assume a broader view of commit-ment, and someone capable of expressing and acting on my desires as he had done with his.

I'm sure my ex-husband regrets not being able to make that tran-sition then, though we haven't discussed it. We are friends now, but *then* it was a war of annihilation, with each of us standing ready to destroy the other out of anger, jealousy, and fear. Ryan and Jetha argue that "rather than endless War Between the Sexes, or rigid ad-herence to a notion of the human family that was never true to begin with, we need to seek peace with the truths of human sexuality."[98] I can follow them right up until the word "truth," which is where I part ways. Although I do not deny that desire often runs counter to good sense, I cannot accept their denial that someone else may define family differently, or that human sexuality is clearly so aligned toward polyamory that we lie to ourselves if we *choose* to be monoga-mous.

I'm probably not the only reader to hesitate when Ryan clarifies the book's position in an interview: "We argue that women aren't whores by nature; they're sluts . . . and we mean that as a compli-ment! In other words, women evolved to have sex for the same reasons men do—because they like it. It feels good. Not because they're trying to get something from men."[99] I'm troubled because the entertainment value of *Sex at Dawn* promotes the book more than the science behind it; the message is that people should fuck more, and that most women want sex with as many men as possible at frequent intervals, and we should just dispense with monoamory because there's no real value in fidelity any more, for either partner.

In a work meant to critique *Sex at Dawn,* self-published by "independent scholar" Lynn Saxon and titled *Sex at Dusk: Lifting the Shiny Wrapping from Sex at Dawn,* I'm unpleasantly surprised to find that her argument lacks the charisma and skill of *Sex at Dawn,* even if it appears to be more solidly grounded in evolutionary biology. I'm not sure if Saxon succeeds, though I can find many positive reviews of Saxon's book by scientists who consistently seem to express disgust and outrage with Ryan and Jethá's text. Bottom line is that I cannot find any information about author Lynn Saxon, other than a Facebook profile, which throws ethos out the window if I'm trying to evaluate and compare the rhetoric of both books' stances on evolutionary theory.

Despite my inability to locate Lynn Saxon's credentials, she successfully casts doubt on Ryan and Jethá's *Sex at Dawn* by helping readers question its validity as an authoritative text. The first such strong point is the distinction that Saxon makes between evolutionary psychology and evolutionary biology,[100] for readers who might not realize that there are separate ways of thinking about human evolution. She also equates Ryan and Jethá's argument to a religious one (like other origin myths) because they single out the story of human beings' evolution, thereby "disconnect[ing] us from the rest of life":

> Readers of *Sex at Dawn* who have little or no previous understanding of evolution and natural selection are unlikely to question arguments about the evolution of human sexuality when only human evolution is addressed, albeit alongside some sparse information from other apes.[101]

Saxon goes on to write that "we tend to easily fall for the idea that natural behaviour and happiness are somehow inter-linked, as if

doing what comes naturally can only be a good thing,"[102] One especially strong articulation of this fallacy is made several pages earlier
in her text and I quote it here at length:

> Whatever we may feel about the "unnaturalness" of human mar-
> riage and monogamy, nature will not give us an alternative happy
> ending to the story of sex—there is in reality an unfortunate clash
> between what we might wish "natural" sex to be and what it in
> fact is. When something is experienced as a natural and imperative
> pleasure it is hardly surprising that it leads to the creation of sto-
> ries which depict some mythological natural world where sex is free
> and easy, the believers arguing that any constraints on their own
> pleasure must be due to "unnatural" forces.[103]

I appreciate the point Saxon is making here because it confirms
what I fear is true of any book that works to justify current social behavior by reaching into the deep and largely unknown past. When I
was in my twenties, disillusioned with patriarchal philosophies and
religious systems, I turned toward radical feminist-centered versions
of history that theorized a golden past of matriarchy. I imbibed the
Old Europe of archaeologist Marija Gimbutas whose Kurgan Hy-
pothesis speculated an original gynocentric culture that was supplanted by androcratic (patriarchal) Proto-Indo-European peoples
known as the Kurgans.

As a fledgling academic, I did not see this as confirmation bias on
my part, to prefer the version of European history that cohered with
my personal religious and political beliefs. Now I see that criticisms
of Gimbutas's work stretch back to the 1960s, by others in her own
field, and as an outsider to archaeology I would be remiss if I did
not acknowledge her controversial status within her discipline. One
can be well-respected, insightful, and contribute great ideas to a field,
but also be fallible. As a layperson and a dabbler in all areas of the
humanities, I must be especially alert to the relativity of academic authority, which exists in close proximity to the canonical versions most
widely accepted. This does not mean we cannot or should not question all of it, including what and why a work or an idea is or is not
canonical. I'm just making an argument for common sense and at-
tentive close readings to discipline-specific forums and conversations.

What I learn from a study of Saxon's text is something I should already know as an academic: two different scholars can read the same text and take away different things, except—Ryan and Jethá's *Sex at Dawn* would not have been a bestseller had there been better quality control over the use of sources, and if the editor had insisted on a peer review process. But what is left then, after Lady Evidence has had her way with a text? What we get as an answer to that question is the force behind Lynn Saxon's *Sex at Dusk*.

In a blisteringly systematic and tedious critique, Lynn Saxon exposes a litany of exclusions between the source texts for *Sex at Dawn* and Ryan and Jethá's conclusions. How anyone can take so much pleasure in the intensity of this analysis is incredible, and I find myself almost willing to go to the sources themselves, to sort out whom to believe. Part of the problem is that I end up trusting Saxon more because she appears to follow the rules of academic argumentation. Ryan and Jethá do not. They increasingly appear as pretenders against the backdrop of anthropological studies and articulations of evolutionary theory that threaten to overwhelm an unprepared reader.

Quite frankly, few readers are going to slog through Saxon's close attention to the stories that Ryan and Jethá omit from the record they relate, or the ways they reorganize their quotations into a tautology for each tale they spin about human sexual evolution. Each conclusion they come to is fraught with omission and jumbling, but reading along as Saxon demonstrates the lacunae is sometimes pretty damn dull. Also, I become fatigued as a reader of a text that is entirely based on criticism, but does almost nothing to entertain me. It isn't until Saxon reaches a kind of fever pitch regarding this history of human sexuality (that Ryan and Jethá posit) that I realize how sardonic she is:

> Ryan and Jethá argue that our ancestors lived in a world "chock-full" of food but chose to stay a bit hungry. The abundant sex would, presumably, have involved thin, barely-fertile women without much in the way of reproductive fat that is stored in the breasts and buttocks of human females. . . . A regular use of infanticide in order to avoid having to go and access those abundant resources needed to feed children or their lactating mothers, and the 'casual

sexual promiscuity' of the *Sex at Dawn* story, unfortunately brings to mind the bawdy Barnacle Bill the Sailor drinking song where the answer to the maiden's question: "What if I should have a child?" is: "We'll smother the bugger and fuck for another." Nice.[104]

I think it's the concluding "Nice" at the end of Saxon's diatribe that is so fascinating. Until now, though she has been wholly critical and sometimes condescending to the argument presented in *Sex at Dawn*, Saxon has not been so openly mocking of the book's conclusion. Propriety aside, she characterizes Ryan and Jethá's perspective as not only naïve, misguided, inaccurate, and skewed, but also— consistent with the tone of the drinking song—grotesquely absurd.

: :

Recently, I began to explore game theory with more energy, even going so far as to begin listening to an audiobook of Ken Binmore's *Game Theory: A Very Short Introduction.* I tend to gain almost nothing from these light forays into fields outside of my own, other than to find phrasal gems that seem worth keeping, as if I actually understand them in their intended contexts. I find also the only book I kept from a philosophy of science course I took in the mid-1990s, John Maynard Smith's *Did Darwin Get It Right?: Essays on Games, Sex, and Evolution.*

I've tried to sell Smith's text multiple times over the years, unsuccessfully. I guess I thought that the book had outlived its relevance to my life. I was never happy with the amount offered by the book buyers, so here it sits, my marginal notes still marking what for me still sounds completely sensible with regard to extrapolations made about human behavior in the context of evolutionary theory. (What I find most interesting now is that this book was the first to introduce the word "meme" into my vocabulary, as an example from Richard Dawkins's book *The Selfish Gene.* The word is now commonplace but dissimilar from its original context.)[105]

The first question that someone might ask is, why do I care? I'm not a scientist, nor am I proficient enough in logic to fully grasp the payoffs and equilibria exemplified by the matrices game theorists use to explain everything from economics to bargaining and military strategy. Still, I'm fascinated by elegant systems, and explanations that appear to offer clean articulations of complex and dynamic ideas. This is what drove me to study philosophy as an undergraduate and much later, a master's student. My dream to be a philosophy professor never quite fulfilled, I look back to the things that inspired me as a young academic, and I want to return to asking those questions.

The drawback of being a more mature academic now is that I see too clearly the fault lines in interdisciplinary dabbling. I will oversimplify and generalize my way into an inductive cul-de-sac. The only legitimacy I will ever have as an essayist is that I do not know, I do not pretend to know, and in fact I will openly ask, *que sais-je?* The reader will justifiably remark that I'm being evasive. Of course there is much worth thinking about with regard to human sexual behavior, and one doesn't have to be an expert in any area to think about any of it.

: :

To the uninitiated, Montaigne can be a challenge to read. One of the first essays of his I read was "On Some Verses of Virgil" in Philip Lopate's landmark anthology *The Art of the Personal Essay*. At the time I was not prepared for his frankness which I misread as arrogance. How dare any man be so direct about his private thoughts concerning women? And how could he think we could ever enjoy extramarital affairs as much as he does? Honestly, I don't know what part of my newly married twenty-three-year-old brain was closed to him through that first encounter. Somehow I mistook him as a misogynist, a lech, and a cheat. This is what I remind myself of when deciding what to have my nonfiction workshop students read. So, they will almost always read his Preface ("To the Reader") with me, aloud, in class; "Of a Monstrous Child," because it's short and odd and in our book; "Of Practice," as a printed handout in Screech's accessible translation, and that's all we have time for.

The one semester I taught an honors seminar entirely on Montaigne to a group of our most promising freshmen, I had them read the following essays in Frame's translation, along with Sarah Bakewell's *How to Live: Or, A Life of Montaigne in One Question and Twenty Attempts at an Answer.*

In this particular order:

1. To the Reader
2. Of Practice
3. Of the Power of the Imagination
4. Of Cannibals
5. Of Smells
6. Of a Monstrous Child
7. Of Presumption
8. By Diverse Means We Arrive at the Same Ends
9. Of Pedantry
10. On Some Verses of Virgil

I chose these works because I thought that learning how to read Montaigne's style gradually was essential to understanding the essays themselves. I also believed that these particular essays showed the range of what Montaigne was capable of: his preface with its intimate, engaging direct address; "Of Practice," because Montaigne relates the narrative of his near death experience, explains why he decided to write essays, and offers the essayist's standard argument against charges of narcissism; "Of the Power of the Imagination," because in it Montaigne offers a legal defense on behalf of his penis, which is classic, and great fun; "Of Cannibals," because his influence on Shakespeare can be discussed in that session, in addition to how open-minded Montaigne was as an ethnographer; "Of Smells" and "Of a Monstrous Child," because they are exemplary "miniature" essays, which get students to thinking about how much the length or commonplace subject of an essay imparts to reflection; I'm not sure any more why I chose essays #7–9 other than I always want students to understand how open-minded Montaigne was for his time, though they almost always have the same reaction I did initially to him, which was negative; and lastly, "On Some Verses of Virgil," the most difficult for them to read and understand.

Since that class I have not taught that essay again. Only one student ever seemed to grasp the full measure of "On Some Verses." In fact, it was through an independent study on the personal essay that I myself came to appreciate the essay at all, and only after my senior student and I spent a total of nine hours dissecting the entire work. We filled a whiteboard with notes, then erased and filled it again. Only through nine separate one-hour sessions of close reading and discussion did we unpack all of the essay, and I came to know the first time, for myself, the value of this kind of devotion. I think of the proverb I'm told comes by way of El Salvador, "The eye of the farmer fattens the cow." In this case, it was certainly sustained close attention to the essay that reaped the rewards I'd never imagined possible before.

"On Some Verses of Virgil" is a longish essay, exceeding 23,000 words, which would probably be a double-spaced Times New Roman 12-point essay of over seventy pages were it to be turned in by one of my students. As boring as they would argue this essay to be, it nevertheless fascinates me every time I encounter it. In Lopate's anthology, the essay stretches over fifty-four pages. Ten percent of the essay rambles about how much it sucks to be old before Montaigne remarks: "But let us come to my theme."

Montaigne's theme is sex, and although I've imagined that acknowledgement enough to entice twenty-somethings to read it, they never do so of their own accord. For whatever reason, knowing what a sixteenth-century man thought about sex isn't enough of a curiosity for them to explore the essay on their own time. Aside from the disappointment I feel toward my students as a group because of this, I admonish myself with the reminder that I missed the essay's delicacy and substance the first time I read it. So—how does one read the essay for the first time, and why am I so preoccupied with it now? My best answer would be that some crisis of sexual/romantic identity precedes understanding of this particular essay, and my preoccupation with it grows as I find many of his complaints in the first ten percent of the essay to be true of my own life, as someone midway through.

Generally I would characterize essayists as a modest lot, the whole of us including myself. Perhaps because the life of the mind so rarely finds expression through the body's knowing, we avoid the most obvious of epistemologies. Or, maybe, I expect too much from writers who must have *something* private left to life in order to enjoy it. I do not want to know the intimate details of someone's married life nor would I want to be included in every erotic dalliance an essay guide might bring me along for. But I do wish that the pleasures most relevant and intriguing to daily life would draw more people to write about them, if for no better reason than to serve levity.

Montaigne points out in "Some Verses" that we are much more freely given over to discussing violence than we are sex, and I recall arguments others have made for why we find violence on television so much more palatable, even for younger viewers, than the occasional naked tit or ass. As a parent, I'll admit freely to this double standard. Why would the act of lovemaking be such an egregious vision compared to a shoot 'em up action film? The collapse of several bodies into puddles of blood or the shimmering skins of lovers entwined and pulsating against the rectangular frame of a comfortable bed? But this is what Montaigne asked so many years ago, himself:

What has the sexual act, so natural, so necessary, and so just, done to mankind, for us not to dare talk about it without shame and for us to exclude it from serious and decent conversation? We boldly pronounce the words "kill," "rob," "betray"; and this one we do not dare pronounce, except between our teeth. Does this mean that the less we breathe of it in words, the more we have the right to swell our thoughts with it?

From a different, more aesthetic and scholarly angle, Montaigne delays his own discussion of human sexuality for several pages because it appears he must lead us in the way he came. He lists all of the "useful thoughts" one could have about the important things in life, but characterizes them as burdens. He realizes that age is making him dull and too serious. "Wisdom has its excesses, and has no less need of moderation than does folly."[106] He says that he is at a point in life where the bad days have overtaken the good in number, and "even the slightest occasions of pleasure" that he encounters, he "seizes."[107]

Aside from his usual gems of aphoristic wit, he is endearing and soft in his wishing: "My philosophy is in action, in natural and present practice, little in fancy. Would I might take pleasure in playing at cobnut or with a top!" His longing to be pleased again with the toys of childhood, to experience the wonder and be given over to "fancy" is only partly figurative. He is willing to grant that each age has its provocations and enjoyments and a young man should be whipped who would fritter his energy away on "wines and sauces." This is the province of Montaigne's time in life, which he shrugs as apropos: "There is nothing I ever knew less or valued less than this. At present I am learning it. I am much ashamed of it, but what should I do?"[108]

He reiterates how youth may have all of the great things of life given that "they are going toward the world, toward reputation; we are coming from it. . . . The laws themselves send us home."[109] This is what he terms the "calamity of old age," and in a pitiable moment he entreats his reader: "If there are any persons, any good company, in country or city, in France or elsewhere, residing or traveling, who like my humors and whose humors I like, they have only to whistle in their palm and I will go furnish them with essays in flesh and bone."[110] Essentially, he's lonely for someone of like mind and willing to travel any distance for the kind of human discourse that would enliven him and help him to "live and be merry."[111]

From this point he appears to draw the circle in tighter. He begins to argue that his own body seems to be against him in his desire to be lighter in his thoughts. The importance of having a good sense of humor (in the contemporary sense as well as the classical) is to him paramount, and he points out that if he (Montaigne) rubs anyone the wrong way with "the license" of his writings, then he accuses them of having much more license in their thoughts.[112] Montaigne makes a case against self-censorship on the basis of what is "shameful" to talk about. He asserts that if it can't be spoken of or written about, it will be repressed. "Those who hide it from others ordinarily hide it from themselves."[113] Furthermore, the diseases of the body, become more visible even as those of the soul "grow more obscure as they grow stronger." He leads us carefully to his strongest point before launching into his study of human sexuality. He desires to publicly confess his deepest thoughts, claiming quite deliciously:

> I am hungry to make myself known, and I care not to how many, provided it be truly. Or to put it better, I am hungry for nothing,

but I have a mortal fear of being taken to be other than I am by those who have come to know my name. . . . I am pleased to be less praised, provided I am better known."[114]

Any personal essayist will sense the manifest quality of this admission, even as a remark which follows turns the gas on under what is at stake in this essay. He claims this "chapter" will put him in the boudoir, and that he likes the society of ladies "when it is somewhat private." Publicly, he finds their company less enjoyable, and this might have pushed me away twenty years ago at my first introduction. But he is saying something much subtler should we catch it. He feels that he is looking back at the pleasures of life more than looking forward. "Here are our last embraces."[115]

: :

I feel that I have in the past few paragraphs pushed the reader farther away from Montaigne and the subject of this essay that I write. Knowing that the subject is sex does not make the buildup better nor does it compel one to invest more work without some pleasure of looking forward. To look only backward at our lives in search of the pleasures there would make most of us turn away.

Robert Atwan's cover essay of "On Some Verses" in *After Montaigne* reaches the best articulation of this painful association when relating his own experience with re-reading the essay "after nearly thirty years, a broken marriage, a sudden solitude, and a dwindling libido."[116] He writes:

> I had been living alone for nearly three years and my early expectations that I would inevitably enter into another intimate relationship had all but vanished. When young you're in some promising social mix nearly all of the time; I didn't realize how different it would be when you reach old age. . . . The hard part of coping with rejection is that it makes you even more sensitive to the possibility of rejection, and—given the law of self-fulfilling prophecy—you start to become assured that to be rejected is your destiny, and thus you grow more hesitant in making any advances or submissions that might invite further rejection.

No matter our age, we feel the ego-crunching sentiment behind these words. We take a turn or two then find all the ways back to another, more hopeful time completely gone. Age is the most powerful of the forces working to divide us from the pleasures of sexual love, but more deeply, our own hopelessness that there are any future delights to be had at all, with anyone, which can settle in us regardless of how old we are. I know young people who are alone because they can find no one who stirs them. I also know of myself that the span of time between sexual interludes grows longer and duller as they become less frequent. I live in a moderately populated small city surrounded by other cities an hour's drive away. But I meet no one whose eyes linger on me, and no one asks for my number. Better to tell myself that I don't want them to. Better to write a whole book about it.

I am not the only single woman I know in her late thirties or early forties who finds herself alone. The friends I have who date, whether online or conventionally, invest a good amount of their lives in being attractive and seeking out partners. I do not. Much of the joy went out of the process these last few years. I hesitate to exercise overly much or diet when my best efforts divide me from dinner with friends or the more accessible pleasure of a latte with breakfast. And really, my last four sexual encounters proved only that men and women fit together rather enjoyably and messily (when they aren't obsessed with catching a disease or becoming pregnant) and that sex in and of itself (fucking) is accessible, though more so for those who are indifferent to romance. This last part is what pains me most, and has turned me increasingly toward solitude.

Atwan's essay is part his own experience and also a focused explication of the major themes that Montaigne take up. I'm pleased to see the many places where Atwan confirms my own thoughts about the work:

> "On Some Verses of Virgil" is the most erotically charged chapter in the Essais. Never shy about the topic, Montaigne writes about sexual matters throughout his essays, but never with an equivalent concentration. The essay has justly been called by James Grantham Turner "perhaps the most profound meditation on sexuality in the Renaissance."[117]

Atwan succinctly states one problem that greets anyone who tries to write about it. "The essay—so wide-ranging it truly resists summary or colligation—then moves suddenly, though strategically, from reflections on our verbal inhibitions to a consideration of love in ancient poetry." The ultimate conclusion is that "erotic poetry can be as sexual as sex itself."[118] This is the ostensible recognition that the essay is indeed about some verses of Virgil's at the same time it deviates wildly into reflecting on sex in general. On the matter of our imaginations and how they play up the power of the written word, I submit evidence from Maggie Nelson's incredible and startlingly lyrical *Bluets,* which spotlights the word "fucking" by her lavish use of it:

> 48. Imagine, for example, someone who fucks like a whore. Someone who seems good at it, professional. Someone you can still see fucking you, in the mirror, always in the mirror, crazy fucking about three feet away, in an apartment lit by blue light, never lit by daylight, this person is always fucking you from behind in blue light and you both always seem good at it, dedicated and lost unto it, as if there is no other activity on God's given earth your bodies know how to do except fuck and be fucked like this, in the dim blue light, in this mirror. What do you call someone who fucks this way?[119]

I take back my earlier remarks about essayists being a modest bunch, on the whole, even as I place the lion's share of responsibility for overturning this crude generalization on Maggie Nelson. *Bluets* is not just about fucking, but about her obsession with the color blue, and the end of a relationship. Lines stand out to me, glittering, aphoristic:

> 71. I have been trying, for some time now, to find dignity in my loneliness. I have been finding this hard to do.
> 72. It is easier, of course to find dignity in one's solitude. Loneliness is solitude with a problem. Can blue solve the problem, or can it at least keep me company within it?
>   . . .

75. Mostly, I have felt myself becoming a servant of sadness. I am still looking for the beauty in that.[120]

I find that reading Nelson's *Bluets* is similar to the pleasure Montaigne finds in reading Virgil, and also oddly mirrors the experience behind his essay. I long for the moments when Nelson remembers the thrill of an encounter or imagines the hottest angle of a phrase. She quotes a passage from William Gass's book *On Being Blue,* which, despite its loveliness, has been supplanted in my appreciation by Nelson's study of the color. She criticizes the way in a particular passage he pushes aside the study of a woman in detail because he has no desire "to see the red lines made by her panties, the pimples on her rump, broken veins like the print of a lavender thumb, the stepped-on look of a day's-end muff." Nelson is sharp in her analysis: "After asserting that the blue we want from life is in fact found only in fiction, he counsels the writer to 'give up the blue things of this world in favor of the words which say them.'"

In a lot of ways, Gass makes a strong point in agreement with Montaigne, that sex is sexier in poetry or prose than in reality, but I think there is more to be said for the way sexuality is written into the question. For a man to desire the fictional woman as opposed to the reality of the woman in his bed? Nelson does not exactly criticize the idea on these terms but on others more aesthetic:

62. This is puritanism, not eros. For my part I have no interest in catching a glimpse of or offering you an unblemished ass or an airbrushed cunt. I am interested in having three orifices stuffed full of thick, veiny cock in the most unforgiving of poses and light. I will not choose between the blue things of the world and the words that say them.[121]

Oddly, I return to Gass's lines that reinforce the idea that "we want to see under the skirt." It jogs a semblance with Montaigne that Atwan remarks on in his essay, when quoting Montaigne:

"Let Martial, as he does, pull up Venus' skirts: things are hidden in order to reveal them more." Although he at one point claims that love is simply a discharging of our vessels, he has nonetheless suggested all through the essay that sex is largely a function of the imagination. Virgil's lines are sexier than sex itself.[122]

Romance, in the context of sexuality, has every mark of being a function of the imagination as well, and is far more detached from the biological reality of human life than fucking. I think too often we confuse the two, as if they always accompany one another. More directly, I think that people part company with one another on the basis that some see the two as linked and many more others are able to see them as separate. An afternoon after she and her lover "fucked for six-hours straight," Nelson remembers the different ways one may claim to be in love with others: "You were on your way to a seaside town, a town of much blue, where you would be spending a week with the other woman you were in love with, the woman you are with now. *I'm in love with you both in completely different ways,* you said. It seemed unwise to contemplate this statement any further."[123]

The reality is that we can love more than one person at the same time and enjoy fucking them as well, but this is aside from the point. The suffering comes in knowing this is not what we wanted at the times that others moved on from us. In this I hesitate to place blame. Having done that too much in the past, I recall the months after my heartbreak with my polyamorous lover and recognize my lack of interest in and enjoyment of sex wherever it appeared: on the radio, in a film, in something I was reading. I no longer felt the joyful spark that told me I had many more loves ahead. ("I don't go to the movies anymore. Please don't try to convince me. When something ceases to bring you pleasure, you cannot *talk* the pleasure back into it,"[124] writes Nelson.) A friend who had been similarly wracked by a heartbreak made the same observation. After a pleasure has been absented from your life, the merest suggestion of it can provoke pain, not pleasure. I am only now in a place where I can read deep into Nelson's bluest lines and enjoy the desire of them:

> When I imagine a celibate man—especially one who doesn't even jerk off—I wonder how he relates to his dick: what else he does

with it, how he handles it, how he *regards* it. At first glance, this same question for a woman might appear more "tucked away" (pussy-as-absence, pussy-as-lack: out of sight, out of mind). But I am inclined to think that anyone who thinks or talks this way has simply never felt the pulsing of a pussy in serious need of fucking—a pulsing that communicates nothing less than the suckings and ejaculations of the heart.[125]

What would Montaigne say is at the root of this quandary, given that his own choices of quotable passages in "On Some Verses" admit no shame when speculating about a woman's desires?

: :

In "Letter from Williamsburg," one of the most mesmerizing and charged essays a friend has ever sent me, Kristin Dombek beautifully captures the pain of a woman who has lost all desire and does not know what is wrong. She is married, has two cats, is unhappy. She fixates on a red armchair where she begins to sit compulsively "for whole afternoons."[126] After leaving her husband and the life that had been so empty, she finds a newness difficult to put into words:

> The first time you feel yourself actually attracted to two people at the same time, in the same place, something very deep is shaken. You want to name the new thing, but you need new syntax to do it. Then you find yourself saying sentences like, "Just relax and let him make you come," or "Don't be nervous, I can tell she really likes you, and I'll help you pick out a wine she'll love," The opposite of the red-chair and dark-room sentences. Sentences that in the speaking give you a feeling that is different in kind from ordinary human love, at least ordinary romantic love.[127]

The most compelling aspect of this essay is her relating of the relationship she finds with a new man, and their sharing of sexual partners. This essay is stunning because she fearlessly uses language that captures the fervor of multipartnered sex in a dimension of self-exploration which is as terrifying as it is thrilling, and gut-wrenchingly honest. She writes about the oddity of a third person, the ways others interpret their roles in the play between regular lovers, and the way lovers see themselves from other angles: "He'd never seen this, the way women can fuck each other; it is quite something to have a man who loves you watch you do it."[128] This kind of experimentation has often struck me as recreational for a time in one's life, but not sustainable if one person entertains the least of a doubt. A man may not want to know how women get along without him; a woman may not be prepared for the way she is satiated by someone other than her mate. Or, how she may only find satisfaction in play with other partners, continually changing.

The music video for Father John Misty's "Nancy from Now On" tells a story that might be a precautionary tale. Two hipster lovers are seen in a hotel room engaging in sadomasochistic play. The man is in the subordinate position as a woman in tall black boots abuses him. She shaves his beard and gives him a haircut. The story shifts to a bar where they feign anonymity and she watches him drink and flirt. During a confusing interlude she has what appears to be an emotional breakdown in the bathroom of the bar. (Is she doubting the fun of their game?) Still, the video ends with them together, somehow graceful and nuanced in the discomfiture of his coming home to bed in the cool light of morning. Where one doubts another might not follow. Someone asks whether this is what she really wants. I have wondered if the desire to be with others is more temporary, more lust than love, despite arguments people make to the contrary, those who find the peace that Dombek sought in freedom and openness.

In "Letter from Williamsburg" the essayist clearly prefers the life she has found though she knows it is more extreme. She does not imagine a greater bond between her and her lover. "He was not really my boyfriend at the time, but that's how it was clearer to talk in certain circumstances."[129] And when he leaves, he does so without ceremony and she does not feel his loss as abnormal or strange.

It is a rare individual who can find pleasure in watching his or her lover attend to another person's desires. But it is perhaps not so rare for people to have fantasized this event at least once, and to have been turned on by their imaginings. It is a twist on human sexuality that we sometimes imagine the scenarios we claim to not want as a way of inciting a deeper response from the core of our rutting instinct. There have been studies done on Internet searches of men and women that reveal shocking desires counter to what people rationally say they want in a long-term relationship. To see the wife fucked by another man, to watch the husband pet and then casually enter a woman that he strokes into a moan. . . . Ryan and Jethá are quick to recognize the ultimate repressed fantasy of human beings, the taboo-breaking daydreams we speak only to ourselves.

We live in a world of consequence and judgment. What we enjoy reading about, what images we search for (bondage, spanking, machines, feet, blindfolds), these are not the material of our lives as we typically live them unless we choose to break with our cultures and our traditions, abandon our searches for monoamorous life partners (or the maintenance of same) in favor of earthly pleasures. (The heated primate howling in the forest for mates, even as they gather around her, eager to taste in turns.) A thin line between one person's deepest desire and another's fear and disgust. Can we say that everything has its context?

: :

The last time I taught "On Some Verses of Virgil" I had just discovered that the man I had been in love with for half a year had a date planned with a woman that week. In fact, the night they were going out, I was leading half a dozen honors students through an abbreviated (two-hour) study of the essay. All that I could think about was polyamory, and so there were so many instances where I felt betrayed by Montaigne, as if he were making the best arguments for not feeling jealousy or not being in a committed relationship and I couldn't disagree. After that night, I couldn't stop thinking about this new angle on the essay I'd not seen before: what seems like an argument for female promiscuity. For a man of his time, it was a radical suggestion. But I would say that even for my own time, some of the ideas in this essay challenge stereotypes and fly in the face of convention.

The first regards marriage, which Montaigne seems to be against, at least, the version which confuses it with love. He argues that we marry "for our posterity, for our family."[130] He sees the benefit in it being an arranged matter, and that procreation be separated from love. Further, he sees a marriage to be more stable the less that it involves passion or ardor. "A good marriage, if such there be, rejects the company and conditions of love. It tries to reproduce those of friendship. It is a sweet association in life, full of constancy, trust, and an infinite number of useful and solid services and mutual obligations."[131]

He says that a wife who relishes her role would not trade it to be her husband's mistress. He also points out that a man would rather shame fall on his mistress than his wife, and given the social roles of marriage, I see why this is indeed so. He claims there "is no finer relationship in our society," but points out that it is still reviled as much as it is essential to civilization. "The result is what is observed about cages: the birds outside despair of getting in, and those inside are equally anxious to get out."[132] This is true in our so-called enlightened times of all kinds of relationships, not just marriage. The cage is not the institution alone, but the place where something of value and beauty is kept. Or so it goes with Maggie Nelson's *Bluets*, #199: "For to wish to forget how much you loved someone—and then to actually forget—can feel, at times, like the slaughter of a beautiful bird who chose, by nothing short of grace, to make a habitat of your heart."[133]

Reading *Bluets,* I sometimes feel overly much the pain of missing someone, of being betrayed, of feeling alone, of being loyal when someone else has not been. It makes it harder to tolerate the philosophy of pleasure which says, simply, let us move along now, to find the next joy, the delights in the next new thing or person. Nelson pushes me to remember the desire, even as it brings me pain. Montaigne forces me to acknowledge the facts of how desire changes, and how what we know about the desires of others also changes. In spite of his opening with the melancholy of old age, "On Some Verses" is a cheerful, provocative essay oriented toward discovering new pleasures while listing the ones he knows. And in some other mode of looking and hearing, *Bluets* commands me to see that one can be sad and disconsolate with longing, but in love with the beauty that persists even after all of the love has been drained out of it: "There is a color inside of the fucking, but it is not blue."[134]

: :

Let us think for a moment about fucking.

Not, I mean, you and I together, but the word and how we feel about it.

I recognize the ways it makes us uncomfortable; for me to write it, for you to read it, and then we think about it, you and I. This is simply, dear Reader, how the relationship works between us. I have brought this word into this space—the word "fuck"—and now I'm struggling to deal with what it means. I see its first appearance in *Bluets* and at that moment I am not offended, but shocked, nonetheless.[135] Nelson lowers the boom and I am smashed against the blue slate floor along with her, *"Fucking leaves everything as it is. Fucking may in no way interfere with the actual use of language. For it cannot give it any foundation either. It leaves everything as it is."*[136]

The riddle is in this word that describes an action, but one that "leaves everything as it is." It does not provide a foundation for anything beyond it, nor does it interfere with language, in that it does not communicate anything beyond itself. It is stasis, but one that I struggle to understand. Does she mean that when we fuck, nothing is changed by having done so? Or does she mean that whatever we had hoped to build through fucking cannot find enough stability to grow? Perhaps that fucking as a practice will not get us anywhere different. We will not call each other differently or seek to define what we have because what we have is fucking. It cannot be a means to an end, but is its own end. What have I done with those I have fucked, except seek to preserve that original desire?

Perhaps, returning to Montaigne, this is why a woman would prefer to be a wife to her husband than his mistress. He claims that he has been a good husband and I believe him, because he admits his own follies so openly regardless: "Licentious as I am thought to be, I have in truth observed the laws of marriage more strictly than I had either promised or expected. It is no longer time to kick when we have let ourselves be hobbled."[137] But he advances the idea further, by continuing to discuss the differences between love and marriage, saying they are "two intentions that go by separate and distinct roads. A woman may give herself to a man whom she would not at all want to have married; I do not mean because of the state of his fortune, but because of his personal qualities. Few men have married their mistresses who have not repented it."[138]

Quoting Isocrates, Montaigne sees love and marriage "at different ends . . . yet in some sort compatible." He continues: "Marriage has for its share utility, justice, honor, and constancy: a flat pleasure, but more universal. Love is founded on pleasure alone, and in truth its pleasure is more stimulating, lively, and keen: a pleasure inflamed by difficulty." His view of the differences make as much sense in our own time as they must have to readers in his own (if they were being as honest with themselves as he was trying to be). He points out this is what makes wives less appealing; they are too available to their husbands, which "blunts the point of affection and desire."[139]

Here is when Montaigne appears to go a slightly off the rails of what one might expect a man of his time to think. He is simpatico with women in all of this, and as a result is forced to admit some uncomfortable truths about the ways men and women are held to different standards. "Women are not wrong at all when they reject the rules of life that have been introduced into the world, inasmuch as it is the men who have made these without them."[140] He also claims that men "treat them inconsiderately" because men know that women "are incomparably more capable and ardent than we in the acts of love." This is only the first part of a ridiculously long and convoluted run-on sentence that basically ends with an example from Juvenal demonstrating the fact that a woman can have sex far more times and with more partners than any man.[141]

To shorten and therefore illuminate the concern, men treat women badly because they know women to be better "in the acts of love" and more capable of multiple "encounters" than they are. This is the reverse of penis envy, I think, as it underscores recognition that a woman could potentially enjoy sex longer and in more sustained ways than men. But this is many hundred years before writing on the orgasm. "In a single sitting a hungry orgasm can consume a man, socks and all. Women take more time," writes Nin Andrews. Or, put a different way, "they are always able to satisfy our needs, whereas it may be otherwise when it is up to us to satisfy theirs," writes Montaigne.[142] This could also direct us to see a biological difference that foments strife between two otherwise loving persons. The doubt that one is enough, or, because a woman does not yet know what she brings into her bed ("they buy a cat in a bag," he writes, regarding the introduction of bodies) . . . well, says Montaigne, "inconstancy is perhaps somewhat more pardonable in them than us."[143] But I skip too far ahead into his thesis.

He points out that women are expected to be both available and desirable to their husbands (which is contradictory, given how desire works), but continent as well, at the risk of "extreme penalties."[144] Men ask women to not want sex, and greatly exaggerate its vice, and yet men do not follow the same rule: "There is no passion more pressing than this, which we want them alone to resist, not simply as a vice of its own size, but as an abomination and execration, more to be resisted than irreligion and parricide; and meanwhile we give into it without blame or reproach."[145]

Despite how hard it is to soothe the earnest desire of the body, he says that men expect women to be "both hot and cold"—that is, a contradiction.[146] And, as he says directly, women are trained "to the ways of love." "Their governesses imprint in them nothing else but the idea of love, if only by continually depicting it to them in order to disgust them with it."[147] In a paragraph just after, he insists that women far exceed men in their knowledge of love, that it is natural to them, and they have no need to learn it. He credits "fear and honor" with keeping the passions of women in check.[148]

Copious examples from antiquity form his proofs that women are as lustful as any man, if not more so, and that in other nations, sexual attitudes were once much freer, with religious practice including sex as a way of preparing for devotions.[149] Montaigne describes rites involving modification of the penis alongside descriptions of Egyptian women wearing wooden dildos "around their neck[s], exquisitely fashioned, big and heavy, according to each one's capacity; besides which the statue of their god displayed one which surpassed in size the rest of the body."[150]

On he talks about the god Priapus and virgins sitting on the lap of his statue at the time of their weddings; he talks of fashion, most likely the codpiece, meant to enhance that part of a man's physique, and in Montaigne's imagination, in "more conscientious ages so as not to deceive people, so that each man alike might publicly and gallantly render an account of his capacity."[151] This culminates in perhaps the best passage in all of the essay, where men and women emerge in their most egalitarian pose, well matched:

The gods, say Plato, have furnished us with a disobedient and ty-
rannical member, which, like a furious animal, undertakes by
violence of its appetite to subject everything to itself. To women
likewise they have given a gluttonous and voracious animal which,
if denied its food in due season, goes mad, impatient of delay, and,
breathing its rage into their bodies, stops up the passages, arrests
the breathing, causing a thousand kinds of ills, until it has sucked
in the fruit of the common thirst and therewith plentifully irri-
gated and fertilized the depth of the womb.[152]

Which leads me to always ask: what is "the fruit of the common
thirst"?

He doesn't stop there. Montaigne laments that women have an
exaggerated idea of the size of a man's penis before she encounters
it in reality, which he blames on pictures that boys leave lying in
the hallways of palaces.[153] More examples from his readings of other
cultures and times demonstrate that nudity has differing effects in
warming or cooling the desires. He thinks it unfair that the imaginations of women have been led so far astray by what they've been
told about men, given that most men would rather their wives not
be as given over to lust as they themselves are.[154]

By placing so many constraints on women to be chaste, Montaigne argues that men make carnality all the more desirable. And in
so doing, men raise the value of a woman who is chaste so that the
more she resists his advance the more he will love her for it. "It costs
her more to give that little than it costs her companion to give her
all."[155] For this, he berates the practice of bragging after one's sexual
exploits: "Truly one must be abject and base in heart beyond measure to allow these tender charms to be so cruelly persecuted, pawed
over, and ransacked by such ungrateful, indiscreet, and fickle persons."[156]

Montaigne's ability to see the double-standard of human sexuality for men and for women helps me to understand him better; not
as a man of his time, since that would be a pale prize for a historical
personage of his caliber, but as a man for all times, who has found
the heart of the conflict between men and women. When he iden-
tifies "the most vain and tempestuous malady that afflicts human

souls," he names it jealousy.[157] Through jealousy, love becomes hatred.[158]

His examples serve up lessons that we should heed, all direct-
ing us away from imagining that we can possess the affections of
another. Here he is led to a tricky prospect: how is it that teaching
women chastity is supposed to hold their desires at bay? What if, he
asks, in their dreams women are led to enjoy all of the many pleasures denied them in waking? And—in a moment of fantasy that
is all Montaigne in spirit, beauty, and whimsy, he suggests that we
"imagine the great rush if a man had the privilege of being borne
swift as a bird, without eyes to see or tongue to tell, into the arms of
each woman who would accept him."[159]

What then? Here the sweetness too . . . that he proposes taking
such opportunities when they are available, without hesitation. And
in this, being delicate to the sting of rejection however it comes, and
from whichever direction, to brave it—but to seize that opportunity, most important, no matter where it leads.

: :

Here, again, reader, I feel that I have misjudged you. The word
"fucking" was a great ring through the nose to lead you into a dry
explication of an essay written four hundred years before you were
born. Perhaps you would have me stall here, and leave you to read
the essay on your own, and I hope you shall. I can give an honest
accounting of what I think he concludes, through insistent banter
with the ancients and all sorts of evidences from cultures as far from
him in geography and period as we are from him, and more.

See, it takes no great mind to plot that men and women in all
times have looked to the exotic (in time or place, it matters not) to
offer examples of better ways to be and to behave (when they weren't
killing each other over those same differences). For Montaigne, a
more natural way of being would have suited, as he states in his preface: "Had my lot been cast among those peoples who are said still
to live under the kindly liberty of nature's primal laws, I should, I
assure you, most gladly have painted myself complete and in all my
nakedness." I think the question is, has he not? Really the trappings

of culture were thrown off far earlier in the essay, when he embarks on a mission of honesty.

The more I read about cultures other than my own, the more I begin to ponder the architecture of my own civilization. "Is there someone who thinks to shackle women by his ingenuity?" asks Montaigne. "What occasion will not be enough for them in so knowing an age?"[160] The essay turns upon the suggestion that given the evils of jealousy, and given that women and men are adulterous regardless, why should chastity be something expected of women? His defense of natural philosophy seems as much a defense of the body and its part in helping us toward our souls: "My page makes love and understands it."[161]

His best, most quotable line—"Let me begin with whatever subject I please, for all subjects are linked with one another"—reminds me that even pages into a digression on writing and books, he is still thinking of sex, which is not separate from his originating thought to seek pleasure as a diversion. His definition of love as "nothing else but the thirst for sexual enjoyment in a desire object" brings down the curtain, lest we thought it more, "nothing else but the pleasure of discharging our vessels," and thus, making "us all equal . . . on the same level the fools and the wise, and us and the beasts."[162]

Sex, as Montaigne's subject, as a subject he claims can be linked to every other, reminds that we still decry the activity of our own generations. ("Are we not brutes to call brutish the operation that makes us?") Further, we shame ourselves for wanting it, and shame the parts that lead us to it. Man is "a stupid production" for hating himself, and in effect denies his own being when he turns away from the pleasures of sex. What's worse, argues Montaigne, we elevate the most heinous parts of human life, and those that would extinguish all pleasure were they unchecked:

> Everyone shuns to see a man born, everyone runs to see him die. For his destruction we seek a spacious field in broad daylight; for his construction we hide in a dark little corner. It is a duty to hide and blush in order to make him; and it is a glory and source of many virtues to be able to unmake him. . . . *We are ashamed of our very selves* [Terence]. We regard our being as vice. . . . What a monstrous animal to be a horror to himself, to be burdened by his

pleasures, to regard himself as a misfortune! . . . Alas, poor man! You have enough necessary ills without increasing them by your invention, and you are miserable enough by nature without being so by art. . . . Just run through a few examples that would illustrate this idea; your life is all made up of them.[163]

As a philosopher, Montaigne often seems ultimate in his instruction. Like anyone who seeks to advance past cultural normativity, his examples come across not much different than any social scientist who points to another way human beings do things. I am not yet tired of reading what a psychologist, a sociologist, an anthropologist, an evolutionary biologist, or a philosopher tell me about how a woman is supposed to be or what a woman is, but *I am* tired of believing that the source of a belief should not be questioned. I do think that each one of us has a peculiar set of motivations behind why we believe what we do that relates to what we want out of the world, and what our own desires might be, apart from what we are told they should be.

Even asking the question of how men and women should be to each other limits the conversation that can be had about sexuality and love to one that is oppressively heteronormative, taken that there are multiple expressions of gender and orientation. Until I have to ask—what can the history of my species's evolution (biological, social, psychological) teach me that would be relevant to my existence now? Can I cast off the yoke of several thousands of years and find my desires acceptable? What Great Geometer made me so flawed that I would continue to be ashamed to be myself?

: :

It is not that I don't find Montaigne reasonable in his thinking. In fact, I'm sure that I infer more into his essay than he intended, yet I feel a strong hand extended to me from his page, inviting me to disagree. The reason I so despised this essay the first time was the line that I could not make less insulting each time I read it: "Why is not one of them seized with desire for that noble Socratic exchange of body for soul, buying a philosophical and spiritual intelligence and generation at the price of her thighs, the highest price to which she can raise them?" He claims that a woman's stupidity can be over-looked if she be beautiful, but that no woman will overlook a man's physical condition in favor of his mind.[164] What I find disheartening is that there were so few women then who could be the woman of his imaginings, and he, perhaps more than any other man, suffered for her absence in his life.

I feel the ironic sting sometimes. I fear that whatever cultivation I have applied to myself has been wasted when all that would qualify me for that most basic of human pleasures is beauty and youth. One I cannot get back and I lose a little more of each day; the other I do not understand, if by understanding I mean to know what others find beautiful in this world. Montaigne is clear about it: "An avowed ugliness and old age is less old and less ugly to my taste than another that is painted and glossed over."[165] The human desire for love does not leave us at a certain age, but continues. And yet, we are at a disadvantage given what is unrecoverable:

> We demand more when we bring less; we most want to choose
> when we least deserve to be accepted. Knowing ourselves for what
> we are, we are less bold and more distrustful; nothing can assure us
> of being loved, knowing our condition and theirs. I am ashamed to
> find myself amid this green and ardent youth. . . . Why should we
> go offering our wretchedness amid this sprightliness?[166]

I do not desire the love of a tender youth, but I am not ready to be passed over by all except the most infirm and unhappy of men! And yet this is a world, has always been a world, where a younger, fitter replacement can be found for the wound that gapes in one's ego. Accusations that one is used by another when the utility of the arrangement was cooperative and mutually beneficial fail to rouse my sympathy. There is no one that takes much from someone who does not offer it first. Every sacrifice we make of ourselves fashions a chain that both parties wear, and a man might buy a woman's time with riches but he can never be sure of where her heart roosts when his eyes are closed.

The artificiality of this—of all that I claim to know about my-self—is that not once has it brought me a pleasure that wasn't in conflict with my mind, or my sense of being in the world. This is something that Montaigne also felt, but met in thoughtfulness after relaying what Agesilaus said, that "wisdom and love cannot live together."[167] Montaigne thinks love to be healthy for one whose soul has grown heavy, and wishes it for himself, saying:

> [Love] would restore to me vigilance, sobriety, grace, care for my person; would secure my countenance, so that the grimaces of old age, those deformed and pitiable grimaces, should not come to disfigure it; would take me back to sane and wise studies, whereby I might make myself more esteemed and more loved, ridding my mind of despair of itself and its employment, and reacquainting it with itself; would divert me from a thousand troublesome thoughts, a thousand melancholy moods, that idleness and the bad state of our health loads us with at such an age; would warm me up again, at least in dreams, this blood that nature is abandoning; would hold up the chin and stretch out a little the muscles and the soul's vigor and blitheness for this poor man who is going full speed toward his ruin.[168]

As painful as love seems to have ended in each case, I cannot say that I would ever withdraw the memory of those joys from my grey vault of past times. Even now, safely ensconced in my easy chair, I recognize how much solace his words bring to my heart, a hopefulness that all things are made lighter by love, and that I need not define it according to any fellow's wit but my own. "Philosophy does not strive against natural pleasures, provided that measure goes with them; she preaches moderation in them, not flight," says Montaigne. I read the flight of my life to and from love, the impertinence of saying that I haven't wanted all that I got. It is not merely that I have a soul but that I have a body and a mind as well.

> May we not say that there is nothing in us during this earthly imprisonment that is purely either corporeal or spiritual, and that we do wrong to tear apart a living man, and that it seems somewhat reasonable that we should behave as favorably at least toward the use of pleasure as we do toward pain?[169]

His reference to the self-perfection saints find through depriva-
tion works equally well here as both a foil to the privileging of pain
over pleasure as a teacher, but also as an absolute tautology given that
pleasure and pain both lead to appreciation of one another. What
Montaigne finds in pleasure, the Tantric philosopher learns and un-
learns. It is the attachment to what must pass that brings suffering.
It is not the pleasure itself which debases us, or the pain alone that
restructures our empathy for others and compassion toward them
and also ourselves. The living man acknowledges what is past and
anticipates what is to come, and pain or pleasure means less than the
fleeing/chasing measure of some existential fugue played on the lap
of night.

It is not the purpose of any part of my culture to define for me
what love is for or whom it should be with; it is not up to the heart
of another how long I should love; the desires of one man are not
the desires of every man I've never known; love can happen simultaneously between several people, or between two, or one for one's
self; we all should be honest with one another at the outset, taking
neither advantage nor too much of another's happiness for granted,
because both might fall short of reality.

Neither my ancestors of a thousand nor those of ten thousand
years live now, and make the decisions I do. Though I hear them
in the mythos of my body, I know their existence to be in part an
echo of what I wish they could have been. I invent my humanity
with every breath, and I wish for it to be a basic human right to seek
knowledge of the self and find it in contemplation, in study, in solitude, and in love.

The ultimate game I think people play with one another is to
cooperate with regards to what we define as "natural." The word is
as laced with ambiguity as the ones we use to describe love, which
we also struggle to impart "naturalness" to. Whether it is natural
for humankind to seek one love or continually be supplanting each
with many, it is natural to ask the question and to also disagree over
the answers. I forgive all of the wrongful suggestions that have been
made to me in this life and I honor the true ones that came at a
price. But I would not hold from anyone else the opportunity to define what is *natural* so long as it contains all that has gone before and
elsewhere.

: :

Early on when studying Bach's *Art of Fugue*, I discovered the contro-
versy surrounding the final contrapunctus in his work: the one that
he supposedly died during writing or left deliberately unfinished,
as Bach scholar Indra Hughes has posited in his 2006 dissertation
titled "Accident or Design?: New Theories on the Unfinished Contrapunctus 14 in J. S. Bach's *The Art of Fugue* BWV 1080." Using
extensive analysis of the numerical correspondences embedded in
the work, Hughes explicates a complex puzzle intended by Bach to
inspire and encourage musicians to complete his masterwork. As
Hughes writes in his abstract, "Bach left the work unfinished deliberately as an invitation to the reader, student or performer to work
out his or her own completion," and "he left a number of clues, hidden to a greater or lesser extent, to indicate that that was his intention and to supply vital information about the content of the
missing bars."[170]

In his first chapter, titled "Bach's Use of Gematria in the Art of
Fugue," Hughes introduces the reader to the meaningful numerological correspondence between letters and words. Were it not for
Hughes's detailed examination of such numerical structures, including that of the BACH motif and the "Bach number" (B (2) + A (1) +
C (3) + H (8) = 14), the reader might find this too tenuous an order
for understanding Bach's work:

> Perhaps no other area of Bach studies has generated such contro-
> versy as the claim that much of Bach's music is founded on, or at
> least contains, hidden numerological or gematric structures or
> meanings. Opinion is sharply divided between those who delight
> in hunting out such numbers in Bach's music and who believe that
> he put them there intentionally, and those who are sceptics and
> who believe that the numbers are either not there or are at best co-
> incidences.[171]

At the very end of my project I learned that in 2010 Loïc Sylvestre and Marco Costa presented evidence in the journal *Il Saggiatore musicale* that *The Art of Fugue* was written to echo the Fibonacci
sequence, the order underlying all life. They illuminate "a mathe-

matical architecture of *The Art of Fugue,* based on bar counts, which
shows that the whole work was conceived on the basis of the Fibonacci series and the golden ratio." Sylvestre and Costa further remark that "a proportional parallelism is also described that shows
how the same proportions were used in varying degrees of detail in
the work."[172] These proportions were also found in Contapunctus
I by Hugo Norden in his analysis appearing in *Fibonacci Quarterly*
2.3 (1964). In their work, Sylvestre and Costa briefly recount the
number of scholars who uncovered similar mathematical correspondences in Bach's work, and they conclude that "the results show that
the whole architecture of *The Art of Fugue* is based on the use of the
Fibonacci numbers and the golden ratios, at least on the level of bar
totals and grouping of the pieces. Since this mathematical architecture encompasses the whole work, with numerous occurrences, the
possibility that they would have arisen *ipso facto* as a consequence of
aesthetic choices or mathematical coincidences can be excluded."[173]

What do these numerical blueprints add to our enjoyment of *The
Art of Fugue*? Or, more precisely, who was *The Art of Fugue* intended
for? I might as well ask, what is this body of mine, or this book, or
this day for, when I ask *why* a piece of music has been written, or *who*
it is for.

The understanding is that Bach wrote *The Art of Fugue* as a con-
tribution to the Correspondierende Societät der musicalischen Wis-
senschaften (Corresponding Society of the Musical Sciences). "The
Society devoted itself to the study of Pythagorean philosophy and
the union of music, philosophy, mathematics and science. Each
member had an oil portrait painted and was expected to contribute a theoretical or practical piece with the aim of developing music
along the philosophical lines of Pythagoras," write Sylvestre and
Costa.[174] Indra Hughes references H. A. Kellner's research in this
area with this anecdote: "It is very likely that Bach intended [*The Art
of Fugue*] to be the third of his submissions to Mizler's society. Bach
waited until he was the 14th member to be admitted to the society,
and to commemorate his admission he had his portrait painted with
14 buttons on his waistcoat; in the portrait he is holding the score
of the 14th of a set of 14 enigmatic canons (the *Goldberg* canons)."[175]

Despite six years of wondering, any conclusion feels as loose, as
easy, as free as ever. Incompleteness is a letting go. One day I stopped

caring what it was for and why it happened. Winning or losing only made sense in the way games make sense, until the rules fall off.

"Ending on a good note" was always how I'd wanted the break-ups to go. So that when we passed on the sidewalk we could tip our hats and walk on. This bitterness has nothing to do with that. No one meets under ideal conditions.

Something else then pulls my attention away—that Bach's name for his work (*Die Kunst der Fuga*) adds up to 158 and Johann Sebastian Bach adds up to 158—"Thus Bach and his work are one and the same."[176] Montaigne said as much, writing in "On Some Verses of Virgil:" "I have done what I wanted. Everyone recognizes me in my book, and my book in me."[177]

I talked about fugue and love and music so much in the beginning, it hurt to think about anything else. Now I want only to think about other things. Perhaps I have hit upon the lateness I've been looking for, this midlife acceptance. The cat sleeps in the window as the light bends away.

NOTES

1. Patrick Madden, *Sublime Physik* (Lincoln: University of Nebraska Press, 2016), 136.
2. Hope Edelman, Paul Lisicky, and Deborah Lott. "Progression by Digression: Multiple Narrative Lines in Creative Nonfiction." Panel presented at the Association of Writers & Writing Program Annual Conference, Boston, March 2013.
3. Madden, *Sublime Physik,* 159.
4. Ibid., 178–79.
5. Douglas R. Hofstadter, *Gödel, Escher, Bach: An Eternal Golden Braid* (Penguin, 1980), 283.
6. Ibid., 719.
7. Indra Nicholas Martindale Hughes, "Accident or Design? New Theories on the Unfinished Contrapunctus 14 in J. S. Bach's The Art of Fugue BWV 1080." PhD diss., University of Auckland, 2006.
8. I think what Bach means here is that he is unable to prevent the living from interpreting his work, or altering it to another purpose. In my copy of *On Late Style: Music and Literature Against the Grain* (Pantheon, 2006) by Edward Said, I found the following scrawled note: "lateness: perhaps also an inability to defend one's own works from being reshaped by others." Edward Said's concept of lateness was suspended with his passing away, although in the chapter titled "The Virtuoso as Intellectual" he draws a complete portrait of Glenn Gould as the chief interpreter of Bach's works. Bach was "a composer whose thinking compositions provided an occasion for the thinking, intellectual virtuoso to try to interpret and invent, or revise and rethink" (130). Said explains this through mention of Laurence Dreyfus's study, *Bach and the Patterns of Invention.* Said underscores the meaning of invention in its "older, rhetorical meaning"

as "the finding and elaboration of arguments" (128), hence his insistence that Gould understood Bach's work to be "both virtuosic and intellectual in the discursive sense at the same time" (127). Said ends by concluding that Gould's performances create "a critical model for a type of art that is rational and pleasurable at the same time, an art that tries to show us its composition as an activity still being undertaken in its performance" (132–33). Gould and Bach were anachronisms of their own times; another gesture toward lateness.

9. *Bending Genre* (New York: Bloomsbury, 2013), 77.

10. Keith Hampton, Lauren Sessions Goulet, Cameron Marlow, and Lee Rainie. "Why Most Facebook Users Get More Than They Give," Pew Research Study. Report: Social Networking, Web 2.0, February 3, 2012, http://www.pewinternet.org/Reports/2012/Facebook-users.aspx?src=prc-headline.

11. "Sean Parker Talks on Facebook Users and Spotify." *Digital Technology: the Tech Portal*, October 19, 2011, http://www.technology-digital.com/social_media/sean-parker-talks-on-facebook-users-and-Spotify.

12. John Dewey, *Art as Experience* (New York: Perigee, 1980), 105.

13. Ibid., 83.

14. "Characteristics of Musical Keys," an online catalogue of historical information about keys and pitches, created by Mickey Koth, music librarian and musician; http://www.biteyourownelbow.com/keychar.htm.

15. "Keys in Music." *Studybass Fundamentals Two, Block: Introduction to Keys and Harmony.* https://www.studybass.com/lessons/harmony/keys-in-music/.

16. Although he is quoted as saying precisely such, the closest language I can find is the following discussion in his "Apology for Raymond Sebond," translated by Donald M. Frame: "Of what is the subtlest madness made, but the subtlest wisdom? As great enmities are born of great friendships, and mortal maladies of vigorous health, so are the greatest and wildest manias born of the rare and lively stirrings of the soul; it is only a half turn of the peg to pass from the one to the other . . . Who does not know how imperceptibly near is madness to the lusty flights of a free mind and the effects of supreme and extraordinary virtue?" Michel de Montaigne, *The Complete Works: Essays, Travel Journal, Letters,* trans. Donald M. Frame (London: Everyman's Library, 2003), 440–41.

17. Stephen Holding, "Self-Centered Erotic Combat," June 10, 2010, https://www.nytimes.com/2010/06/11/movies/11coco.html.

18. Igor Stravinsky, *Poetics of Music: In the Form of Six Lessons* (Cambridge, MA: Harvard University Press, 1942).

19. Ibid., 4.

20. Ibid., 7.

21. Ibid.

22. Ibid., 140.

23. *Igor Stravinsky: Composer,* directed by János Darvas (Munich: Metropolitan, 2001), 3 min and 44 sec. My transcribed notes identify the time but may differ from the actual film. About the film: "Assembled entirely from black-and-white archival footage, *Igor Stravinsky: Composer* is an amazing work that allows us glimpses of the maestro's fascinating relationships with many of the century's other great artists and politicians," says G. Cahill of the California Film Institute.
24. Stravinsky, *Poetics of Music,* 63.
25. Ibid., 53.
26. Stravinsky, *Poetics of Music,* 63.
27. *Igor Stravinsky: Composer,* 16 min 29 sec.
28. Stravinsky, *Poetics of Music,* 69–70.
29. Ibid., 63.
30. Ibid., 76.
31. Ibid., 11.
32. Ibid., 83.
33. Ibid., 12.
34. Ibid., 64–65.
35. Ibid., 83.
36. Ibid., 86.
37. Ibid.
38. Ibid., 87.
39. *Igor Stravinsky: Composer,* 11 min 43 sec.
40. Ibid., 12 min 15 sec.
41. Stravinsky, *Poetics of Music,* 88.
42. Ibid., 15.
43. Ibid., 79.
44. Ibid., 65.
45. Ibid., 63.
46. Ibid., 64.
47. Ibid., 70.
48. Ibid., 56.
49. Stravinsky, *Poetics of Music,* 57.
50. Ibid., 80–81.
51. Ibid., 65.
52. Ibid., 50.
53. Ibid., 51.
54. Ibid.
55. Ibid., 53–54.
56. Ibid., 140–141.
57. Ibid., 54.
58. Ibid., 36.
59. Ibid.
60. Ibid.

61. Ibid., 54–55.
62. Ibid.,, 55.
63. Ibid.
64. Ibid., 140.
65. Michel de Montaigne, "Of Glory," in the *Essays of Montaigne,* trans. Charles Cotton.
66. Montaigne, "Of Glory," 34.
67. Philip Lopate, Introduction, *The Art of the Personal Essay: An Anthology from the Classical Era to the Present* (New York: Anchor, 1995), xxv–xxvi. "If, however, the essayist stays at the same flat level of self-disclosure and understanding throughout, the piece may be pleasantly smooth, but it will not awaken that shiver of recognition—equivalent to the frisson in horror films when the monster looks at himself in the mirror—which all lovers of the personal essay await as a reward."
68. Stephen King, *Danse Macabre* (New York: Gallery Books, 2010), 49.
69. Stravinsky, *Poetics of Music,* 34.
70. Ibid., 35.
71. Ibid., 73.
72. Ibid., 73–74.
73. Ibid., 74.
74. Ibid., 37.
75. *Igor Stravinsky: Composer,* 2 min 58 sec.
76. Ibid., 46 min 7 sec.
77. Ibid., 3 min 30 sec.
78. Ibid., 7 min 13 sec.
79. Stravinsky, *Poetics of Music,* 25.
80. Ibid., 28.
81. Virginia Tufte, *Artful Sentences: Syntax as Style* (Cheshire, CT: Graphics Press, 2001), 9.
82. Stravinsky, *Poetics of Music,* 30.
83. Ibid., 31.
84. Ibid., 32.
85. Ibid.
86. Ibid., 19.
87. Ibid., 24.
88. Martin J. Osborne and Ariel Rubinstein, *A Course in Game Theory* (Cambridge, MA: MIT Press, 1994), 15.
89. R. Duncan Luce and Howard Raiffa, *Games and Decisions: Introduction and Critical Survey* (New York: Dover, 1957), 91.
90. Ibid., 91.
91. From an email dated May 23, 2016.
92. Laura Kipnis, *Against Love: A Polemic* (New York: Vintage, 2004), 52.
93. The last time I counted, he says "a thousand times" exactly twenty-three times over.

94. Christopher Ryan and Cacilda Jethá. *Sex at Dawn: How We Mate, Why We Stray, and What It Means for Modern Relationships* (New York: Harper Perennial, 2012), 12. Kindle Edition.

95. Ibid., 50.

96. Ibid., 279.

97. Ibid., 310.

98. Ibid.

99. Chris Ryan in a 2010 podcast interview with Dan Savage.

100. Lynn Saxon. *Sex at Dusk: Lifting the Shiny Wrapping from Sex at Dawn* (CreateSpace), 11. Kindle Edition.

101. Ibid.

102. Ibid., 48.

103. Ibid., 32.

104. Ibid., 223–24.

105. John Maynard Smith. *Did Darwin Get it Right?: Essays on Games, Sex, and Evolution* (New York: Springer, 1988), 108.

106. Montaigne, "On Some Verses of Virgil," trans. Donald Frame, in Philip Lopate, *The Art of the Personal Essay*, 59.

107. Ibid., 60.

108. Ibid., 60.

109. Ibid., 60.

110. Ibid., 61.

111. Ibid.

112. Ibid., 62.

113. Ibid., 63.

114. Ibid., 65.

115. Ibid.,

116. Robert Atwan, "Of Sex, Embarrassment, and the Miseries of Old Age," in *After Montaigne*, eds. David Lazar and Patrick Madden (Athens: University of Georgia Press, 2015), 174.

117. Ibid., 163.

118. Ibid., 164.

119. Maggie Nelson, *Bluets* (Seattle: Wave Books, 2009), 18–19.

120. Ibid., 28–29.

121. Ibid., 24–25.

122. Atwan, "Of Sex, Embarrassment, and the Miseries of Old Age," 170.

123. Nelson, *Bluets*, 46.

124. Ibid., 66.

125. Ibid., 72.

126. Kristin Dombek, "Letter from Williamsburg," in *Best American Essays 2014*, ed. John Jeremiah Sullivan (New York: Scribner, 2014), 24.

127. Ibid., 28.

128. Ibid., 26.

129. Ibid., 25

130. Montaigne, "On Some Verses of Virgil," 67.
131. Ibid., 69.
132. Ibid.
133. Nelson, *Bluets,* 79.
134. Ibid., 19.
135. Ibid., 7.
136. Ibid., 8.
137. Montaigne, "On Some Verses of Virgil," 70.
138. Ibid., 71.
139. Ibid.
140. Ibid.
141. Ibid., 72.
142. Ibid., 101.
143. Ibid.
144. Ibid., 72.
145. Ibid.
146. Ibid.
147. Ibid., 73.
148. Ibid., 74.
149. Ibid.
150. Ibid., 75.
151. Ibid., 76.
152. Ibid.
153. Ibid., 77.
154. Ibid.
155. Ibid., 79.
156. Ibid., 80.
157. Ibid., 80–82.
158. Ibid., 82.
159. Ibid.
160. Ibid., 85.
161. Ibid., 90.
162. Ibid., 93.
163. Ibid., 95–96.
164. Ibid., 111.
165. Ibid., 110.
166. Ibid., 108–09.
167. Ibid., 106.
168. Ibid., 108.
169. Ibid.
170. Hughes, "Accident or Design?," 3.
171. Ibid., 10.
172. Loïc Sylvestre and Marco Costa, "The Mathematical Architecture of Bach's 'The Art of Fugue,'" *Il Saggiatore musicale* 17, no. 2 (2010): 179.

173. Ibid., 189.
174. Ibid.
175. Hughes, "Accident or Design?," 26.
176. Ibid., 24. "Kellner concludes from this that the title 'Die Kunst der Fuga' is the correct title for the work. It does however appear to escape his attention that 1+5+8 = 14."
177. Montaigne, "On Some Verses of Virgil," 92.